T0342059

# Business
# Exit Planning

Founded in 1807, John Wiley & Sons is the oldest independent publishing company in the United States. With offices in North America, Europe, Australia and Asia, Wiley is globally committed to developing and marketing print and electronic products and services for our customers' professional and personal knowledge and understanding.

The Wiley Finance series contains books written specifically for finance and investment professionals as well as sophisticated individual investors and their financial advisors. Book topics range from portfolio management to e-commerce, risk management, financial engineering, valuation and financial instrument analysis, as well as much more.

For a list of available titles, please visit our Web site at www.WileyFinance.com.

# Business Exit Planning

*Options, Value Enhancement,
and Transaction Management
for Business Owners*

## LES NEMETHY

John Wiley & Sons, Inc.

Published by John Wiley & Sons, Inc., Hoboken, New Jersey.

Published simultaneously in Canada.

For general information on our other products and services or for technical support, please contact our Customer Care Department within the United States at (800) 762-2974, outside the United States at (317) 572-3993 or fax (317) 572-4002.

Wiley also publishes its books in a variety of electronic formats. Some content that appears in print may not be available in electronic books. For more information about Wiley products, visit our web site at www.wiley.com.

*Library of Congress Cataloging-in-Publication Data:*

Nemethy, Les.
    Business exit planning : options, value enhancement, and transaction management for business owners / Les Nemethy.
        p. cm.—(Wiley finance series)
    Includes index.
    ISBN 978-0-470-90531-9; ISBN 978-1-118-02297-9 (ebk); ISBN 978-1-118-02295-5 (ebk); ISBN 978-1-118-02296-2 (ebk)
    1. Sale of business enterprises.  I. Title.
    HD1393.25.N46 2011
    658.1'64–dc22

                                                                                            2010053528

Printed in the United States of America

10   9   8   7   6   5   4   3   2   1

*To my father*

# Contents

# Preface

**O**ver the years, I have spoken to thousands of business owners and investors on the subject of buying or selling businesses. It has become apparent to me that there is a real need for business owners to better understand how to go about planning and managing their **Business Exits**. While there are thousands of books on the subjects of Mergers & Acquisitions (M&A) and corporate finance, these are generally aimed at M&A or finance professionals, not at business owners. This book is designed to fill that gap. Targeted to business owners, it covers both **Business Exit Planning** *and* **Transaction Management**.

This is not a textbook. It does not go into tremendous detail on any subject, but rather gives a bird's eye view of what you, as a business owner, need to know to plan and execute your business exit. Entire tomes could, and indeed have been written about Management Buyouts, Initial Public Offerings (IPOs), valuations, and so on. But in giving very brief introductions to these and many other subjects, my goal is to give you enough information (in an easily readable format) so that you can decide for yourself whether a particular subject warrants further investigation.

The generality of this bird's eye view is also reflected in the fact that I don't analyze the subject of planning and executing Business Exits within the context of any particular legal jurisdiction. I will look at universal themes and issues, rather than provide a detailed roadmap for a particular company within a particular legal jurisdiction. It has been a challenge to give meaningful advice in the absence of the legal context in areas like tax or estate planning. Nevertheless, most of the content should be applicable to any country; but please, consult legal counsel and other advisors before taking any concrete action.

I have done my best to illustrate the principles set out in this book with real-life examples. I use miniature case studies, based on personal experience, throughout the text. The majority of these are in the context of **Transactions** or assignments carried out by my firm, Euro-Phoenix Financial Advisors Ltd. The case studies themselves generally don't reveal sufficient information to identify the companies or individuals in question. Although our Confidentiality Agreements have expired in the majority of instances, we respect the confidentiality of our clients above and beyond the minimum legal requirement. In one or two cases where I thought the identity might be of particular interest, I obtained the consent of the company.

I do not claim originality for the ideas expressed in this book, as can be seen from the sources quoted in the Endnotes. What will be of use to you, as a business owner, is the bird's eye view and the way in which the information is synthesized and illustrated with relevant case studies and a glossary of frequently used technical terms.*

This book is designed for owners of what I would call 'mid-sized' businesses. These are typically businesses that have minimum values in the range of $10 million to $100 million, although I am the first to admit that this range is arbitrary. Businesses with values smaller than $10 million often resort to business brokers rather than corporate finance or investment-banking-type advisors. Some do not use advisors at all (other than legal advisors) because the advisory fees would consume a large percentage of the Transaction revenues. It is particularly challenging for owners of such small businesses to obtain quality advice at a reasonable cost, given the size of the deal in question. This book is a good starting point.

Businesses with values larger than $100 million are at the other extreme: they typically have numerous investment banking or corporate finance relationships, and are usually more sophisticated in their corporate finance knowledge than small and mid-sized firms.

As already mentioned, this book deals with two major subjects: *Business Exit Planning* (presented in detail in Part I), followed by *Transaction Management*—what a business owner needs to know in managing the exit Transaction—(covered in detail in Part II).

I have heard the argument expressed that a book on Business Exit Planning should not cover Transaction Management. After all, there are many other methods of exiting your business than an outright sale. There are two reasons why I ultimately opted to include Transaction Management in a tome on Business Exit Planning. First, for mid-sized businesses, sale is probably the most frequent form of exit, and in a chess game it is always good to plan several moves or alternatives in advance. And second, exits other than sale (such as Management Buyout or transferring ownership to the next generation) will also involve a Transaction of sorts. A book that covers both Business Exit Planning and Transaction Management should equip you, the business owner, with a full overview of what's involved in exiting your business.

That does not mean that this book covers everything you need to know. As the saying goes: the larger the circumference of light, the larger the

---

* Terms included in the glossary appear in **bold** when first used in a chapter.

circumference of darkness around it. Part of the value of this book is that it will make you more aware of possible blind spots, where expertise is lacking within your organization, or where you may need to seek further advice.

Just as planning the construction of a house takes longer and is not as dramatic or exciting as seeing the house grow before your eyes, so too, you will find that it may take some effort to work your way through the planning phase, whereupon you will be rewarded with a faster and better construction. I have built a number of houses, and have always found that the planning (architectural drawing, permits, etc.) takes two or three times longer than the actual construction itself. If you persevere and invest time to understand Part I, you are likely to achieve a better result with Part II.

Should you wish to contact me, please feel free to do so at the email address following, or follow me on Twitter or on my web sites.

Les Nemethy
Email:                      LNemethy@europhoenix.com
Twitter:                    www.twitter.com/lnemethy
Euro-Phoenix web site:      www.europhoenix.com

# Acknowledgments

I am grateful to the many friends and colleagues who contributed to this book and helped to make it a reality:

I would like to thank my colleagues at Euro-Phoenix: Iain McGuire, who reviewed the manuscript and contributed to the sections on Estate Planning and Taxation; László Nagy, who reviewed the entire document and, along with Daniel Blazic contributed primarily to the sections on Business Plan and Valuation; Andras Hanak, who reviewed the manuscript from a legal perspective; and Aron Negyesi, who assisted with research.

I would also like to thank those who contributed to editing the manuscript: Mary Murphy, Simon Mort, and Christine Ro, as well as Erika Szabó, who made numerous constructive suggestions with respect to the book.

Special thanks go to Paul Garrison, for providing some of the impetus for writing this book (and also reviewed the document), as well as to Dante Roscini, Brian Hoyes, and Hartmut Emans for their useful suggestions; to Doug Robbins for his insights into the M&A industry over the years; and to José Manuel Ferrer for providing information on the Codorniu company.

I would like to give special thanks to John and Tamara Scurci for their hospitality on the islands of Montserrat and Virgin Gorda (of the British Virgin Islands) and for making the writing of this book possible in such wonderful locations.

# Disclaimer

This book is designed to provide business owners with general concepts for preparing and executing Business Exits. Every business, however, is different, faces different challenges, has different objectives, and is in a different legal jurisdiction. This book is not intended to encourage 'do it yourself' activities when it comes to selling a business or planning an exit. None of the statements set out in this book should be relied upon as professional advice to form the basis of a Business Exit. Readers are urged to seek legal, accounting, tax, financial, and other professional advice, as appropriate.

# Foreword

For any company, a change in ownership structure is an extraordinary event and the decision regarding when and how to exit the business is among the most important that the controlling shareholders have to make. The exit can take many forms: will it be total or partial? Will it be through the public or the private markets? Will it be through the injection of new capital or the sale of existing shares?

These decisions are made more involved by the presence of multiple shareholders. But for many small and medium-sized businesses, where the ownership structure is less complex, the decision maker is often not only the main shareholder but also the main executive and the operating leader. He or she may have founded and grown the business or inherited it from previous generations, making the responsibility for the decision all the more burdensome.

The result is that a change in ownership is generally emotionally charged and has far-ranging consequences for the business owner from a professional, financial, and personal standpoint. The decision impacts the individual and his or her estate, the company, its management, its employees, and all of the other entities associated with the business. If the owner is also the manager, the issues of transition and of his or her involvement after a financial transaction are central to the very continuity of the firm.

In more than two decades as an international investment banker I was able to verify that the issues and the process shareholders face in a Business Exit are remarkably similar regardless of size, sector, or geographic location. Yet even with these similarities, planning and managing an exit is a highly complex undertaking.

The consequence for smaller enterprises is that this is not a do-it-yourself endeavor. Working with advisors is inevitable in order to deal with the process efficiently, identify and negotiate with the right counterparties, follow the appropriate procedures, abide by the varying rules and regulations, and conduct a transaction that leads to the best outcome.

This book not only helps to maximize value, but also assists with the countless nonfinancial aspects which must be examined in the overall scheme of business exit. An entire industry of advisors revolves around shareholders who are planning a transaction. Large companies tend to have established relationships with investment banks and produce deals of sufficient size to allow them to receive high quality advice on a regular basis. But high quality advice is costly and can be challenging for owners of smaller businesses to obtain. This book represents a very good place to start.

Many books have been written regarding mergers and acquisitions, initial public offerings, leverage buy outs, and other forms of partial or total change in ownership. This book is unique in several respects: it is primarily written for owners rather than for advisors, it is practical rather than theoretical, it synthesizes complex information in an engaging and easy-to-read manner, and it is rich in real-life case studies.

I have known Les Nemethy for 40 years and I have followed his career as an entrepreneur, as a government official in charge of Hungary's privatization program as a senior manager at the World Bank, and then as an investment banker. His successful firm, Euro-Phoenix Financial Advisors Ltd., has given advice to hundreds of companies, making his experience particularly relevant to the topic and the case studies so insightful.

The book gives a very complete overview of the issues involved in business exit planning, identifies the critical decision making points, describes how to choose and work with advisors, warns about the possible mistakes in the process, and explains how to avoid these mistakes. I believe it is one of the best and fastest ways of getting a clear grounding on one of the most important and complex processes that a shareholder will face in the life of his or her company.

Dante Roscini
Senior Lecturer, Harvard Business School
Former Global Head of Capital Markets,
Merrill Lynch

# Introduction
## The Challenge of Exiting Your Business

*All the world's a stage,*
*And all the men and women merely players.*
*They have their exits and their entrances;*
*And one man in his time plays many parts ...*
—William Shakespeare (1564–1616)
*As You Like It*, Act II Scene VII

Anyone can buy or create a company. But how do you exit successfully? A **Business Exit** is not just a simple question that you might ask yourself as a business owner: Do I exit—yes or no? Most business owners find the issue excruciatingly difficult to grapple with because it is not just one decision; rather, in most cases, there are many interrelated decisions to be made, such as:

- What will you do with your free time after exiting? What new purpose will your life take on?
- How much money will you receive upon exit? Will this be enough to cover the objectives that you'd like to achieve? If you are nearing retirement age, will this be enough to cover retirement expenses, leave a legacy for your family, and cover possible medical costs?
- What will happen to your staff, clients, and business partners?
- What is the best timing for your exit, given the economic cycle of your country and industry, as well as the growth curve of your company?
- What will be the best form of exit (e.g. sale, going public on a stock exchange, selling to management, or transferring to your children)?
- How will you preserve confidentiality during the exit process, to ensure that your business isn't damaged?

- How will you actually run the process and conduct a **Transaction**? What kind of advisors will you need? Who will you use?
- How will you minimize (legally avoid) taxes?
- How will you help ensure the continuity of your company? Should you seek or be available for a post-exit role in assisting your company to manage this continuity?
- How will you invest any proceeds from a Business Exit?

> Hesitation is normal, but procrastination may be dangerous.

You're not alone: most business owners hesitate or even procrastinate when making decisions about Business Exits. The sheer impact of the decisions may give pause; the timing may not be perfect (it seldom is!); or you may simply not be prepared, emotionally or psychologically, to exit. Hesitation is normal, but procrastination may be dangerous. The best time to plan your exit is when you don't have to exit. If you really have to exit, it may already be too late.

In Box 1.1, I share a personal experience that marks the beginning of my dedication to this subject and graphically illustrates the danger of ignoring or postponing the planning of a Business Exit, as well as the fuzzy thinking that often accompanies it.

From my conversations with thousands of business owners over the years, I know that most either procrastinate in developing an exit plan or suffer from similarly fuzzy thinking. It's natural to avoid thinking about matters that are unpleasant, such as death or major life changes. Most business owners are so caught up in the day-to-day aspects of managing their businesses that there is a tendency to prioritize matters that are urgent over matters that are important. Business Exit Planning consumes a considerable amount of time. It also requires input from multiple disciplines. So the tendency to procrastinate is not surprising. According to a 2008 UK study, 30 percent of all business failures are due to succession failure.[1] And of those owners who do manage to exit, a large number do not maximize the full potential of their Business Exits.

Getting into a business is considerably easier than getting out of one. Sir Edmund Hillary may not have been the first man to make it to the top of Mount Everest; there may have been several before him. More precisely, Hilary was the first man to make it down from the summit alive. Making it up a mountain, when you are physically and mentally geared toward reaching the top, may be easier than making it down, when it is much easier to slip and fall.[2]

## BOX 1.1   AN ENGINEERING CONSULTING COMPANY

In 1968, my father founded an engineering consulting company, based in Toronto, Canada. By the 1980s, it had grown to more than 130 engineers, having served clients in more than 40 countries. A number of competitors had approached my father on several occasions with a view to buying the company, but he rejected all approaches in a rather summary fashion. My father was a dynamo; a self-made man who was fiercely proud of his independence.

In 1989, one minuscule event had an enormous impact: a tiny blood vessel in the back of his brain burst. The stroke disabled his speech for months, clouded his judgment, and left his body partially paralyzed. He was just 67 years old at the time. Meanwhile, his business, already feeling the effects of a recession, went into a tailspin. It was unable to attract new clients, began losing existing clients—not to mention staff—and started piling up serious losses.

A few months after his first stroke, my father temporarily regained sufficient judgment and speech to consider what he believed to be his three options. First, he considered hiring someone to run the business, but could not find anyone who had the many competencies required, or who could be trained quickly. He had neglected to groom a successor inside the company. Second, he could find a buyer for the business, but he quickly realized that without being available himself for at least a year or two to ensure an orderly transition, even if the company could restore positive cash flow, it would have no real market value. Given his state of health, this was a non-starter. His third option—or as he found out the hard way, his only real option—was to shut down the business. All other options were illusions. The liquidation took two months and was very painful. The remaining staff members were let go, assets were sold for a pittance, and the business was wound down in as orderly a fashion as possible. Instead of providing cash, the honoring of all corporate liabilities absorbed a significant portion of his remaining personal cash.

No one was more devastated by the shutdown than my father. Twenty years of incredibly hard work had been frustrated by the momentary misbehavior of one tiny blood vessel. He deeply regretted that his company did not survive him (he had harbored a vague desire that I take over from him, even though I was not an engineer and had repeatedly declined his offer). Laying off staff pained him greatly. He viewed the shutdown as a colossal waste of his life's work.

*Continued*

> Because the majority of his net worth had been tied up in his company—which at its peak may have theoretically been worth many millions of Canadian dollars—he realized that not only would he be unable to bequeath much to his family, but also that his remaining personal assets were insufficient to provide for his own nursing care in the medium to long term. My father passed away in 1993.

My point is not that every business owner should exit the business, but that every business owner should have *a plan* to exit the business. When you plan for the ascent, you should also plan for the descent. (And you might also plan for an early descent, in case of bad weather.)

> Are the steps I am taking to build my business enhancing the value of my business from an investor's perspective?

Most business owners only plan for the ascent, and hence find the descent—the exit—extraordinarily difficult. This is partly because many business owners usually look at running their businesses and exiting their businesses as completely separate, unrelated, and distinct acts, not realizing that the two are inextricably linked. A Business Exit should be a culmination of the process of building a business, part of a natural continuum. From inception, and while building the business, you should always have the endgame in sight. You should continually ask yourself: *Are the steps I am taking to build my business enhancing the value of my business from an investor's perspective?*

Many business owners never succeed in the exit, at tremendous cost to themselves and to their businesses. Others do so in a way that either fails to best achieve their personal objectives as shareholders or fails to find the right type of investor for the business. Many owners who do exit leave a lot of money on the table—all because they did not properly plan and execute their Business Exits. As the saying goes: failing to plan is planning to fail. Despite the huge stakes involved, many business owners spend more time planning their holidays than the long-term future of their businesses.

Fortunately, there is an emerging body of knowledge on Business Exit Planning that helps you plan for the descent. There are an overwhelming number of options available to owners of mid-sized businesses—options for those who want to exit in the financial sense, but remain active in the business; options for those who no longer want to be active, but may want to remain invested in the business; and options for those who want to sever ties completely. There are options for owners who seek an immediate exit, and options for those who prefer a staged exit over time. Fortunately for owners of mid-sized businesses, there is great interest in mid-sized companies, and an enormous amount of capital has been mobilized to invest in the mid-market. Hence, there are many options available!

Once you, as the owner, have decided to exit (and have made all those exit-related decisions set out at the beginning of this Introduction), proper execution of a Transaction is vital to success. This involves a different but related set of skills, which, using the title of Donald Trump's book, I call *the art of the deal*[3]—how to obtain the best possible price and terms. But even here, it is not just a question of agile negotiation, but also of painstaking preparation. What kind of process will be involved in the sale? What kind of information disclosure do investors receive? You will need to prepare extensive information disclosure. Will the investors uncover any surprises during **Due Diligence**? How well can you satisfy their Due Diligence concerns? These are just some of the issues encountered. The artful negotiation is the tip of the iceberg—seven-eighths of the iceberg, the preparation, is submerged under water, invisible.

> It is not just a question of agile negotiation, but also of painstaking preparation

A properly planned and executed exit is usually linked to a liquidity event that unlocks your wealth so that it may be used for your retirement, to lay the financial foundation for your family members, or for other purposes, while ensuring an orderly succession for the governance and continuity of your business.

There are millions of business owners the world over who have faced or are facing similar issues concerning a Business Exit. As I've said before, you're not alone. Many have never exited a business before, and are perhaps not even sure where to turn for advice.

Most business owners are unsung heroes of society. Only a few business owners are widely celebrated or acquire superstar status. But as a business owner, you have probably created or grown an organization that provides value to society, provides jobs and revenue for employees, and provides work for suppliers. Most wealth creation is driven by business owners. It would be a terrible shame not to let the benefit of these superhuman efforts reverberate through future generations, as well as benefit families and loved ones. That will require Business Exit Planning followed by a successful implementation of the plan.

While there are serial entrepreneurs who spawn companies with amazing frequency, for most business owners exiting is a once-in-a-lifetime experience; hence few business owners really understand at the outset what is involved. May this book help you in your endeavors; may it help you visualize your destination and how to get there; and may it make your journey more enjoyable and successful.

## THREE OVERARCHING THEMES

Let's now take a quick look at three overarching themes I will develop throughout the book:

### A Successful Exit Is Seldom Spontaneous, but the Result of a Carefully Prepared Process

A systematic, carefully prepared exit that is planned, initiated, and controlled by the owner (what I like to call a *systematic approach*) will almost always yield a better result than a spontaneous process (an *ad hoc approach*). An ad hoc approach typically occurs where an investor approaches the owner with a spontaneous offer, or there is a chance encounter that results in a negotiation.

Many business owners believe their business is worth more if an investor approaches them. More often than not this is a very big mistake, as we will see later.

The following scene has been played out countless times: an investor approaches the business owner with an offer that seems attractive. They go out for a wonderful lunch or dinner—the great seduction scene. The personal chemistry is excellent, consensus emerges quickly, and the parties map out a deal on the back of a napkin. They shake hands on the general framework of a deal, perhaps even agree on the value of the business, and depart thinking that the deal is done, subject only to some minor details.

One set of answers leads to another set of questions.

Then the investor starts his or her Due Diligence. A trickle of questions turns into an endless stream. One set of answers leads to another set of questions. The stream turns into a torrent. The barrage of questions puts serious pressure on company management. The investor becomes frustrated with the slow pace at which the incomplete information is provided, and with the ambiguity or inaccuracy, or perhaps even contradictory nature, of the information received. The owner becomes frustrated with the resources consumed, and often misconstrues the questions as a lack of trust or failing commitment on the part of the investor. If the initial waves of questions are answered satisfactorily, the investor goes on to appoint legal advisors and auditors, who then unleash further extensive waves of newer and even more complicated and more detailed questions. Whole teams of advisors descend upon the company, taking information demands to new heights. Company management is under huge stress—after all, managers have a business to run, yet satisfying the investor turns into more than a full-time job. Tensions mount. More often than not, negotiations break off—sometimes in an emotional or dramatic showdown—or the parties may just give up from exhaustion or frustration. If you have tried an ad hoc or spontaneous process, this might sound familiar.

The bottom line is that it takes many months of preparation by most companies to face an investor's informational onslaught. The fundamental reason for the frequent failure of the ad hoc approach is the seller's lack of preparation. Most business owners dramatically underestimate the amount of preparation required for a Transaction, as well as the investor's informational needs.

The process of Business Exit Planning, as described in this book, will help you, as an owner, to extensively prepare yourself prior to your first encounter with an investor. The preparation occurs at two levels: first, you will have much clearer expectations, in your own mind, concerning what you require or expect from an investor; and second, you will have done much more to prepare the type of disclosure the investor will require *prior* to the first encounter.

The investor's expectation is that you will have information at your fingertips, or that you can prepare it practically overnight. If you don't, the investor will most likely conclude that your company is not that well managed, and may possibly use this as a lever to discount the valuation.

If you enter into a sale process when an investor approaches you, in all likelihood you will not have selected the right moment from the point of view of preparing your business and having created sustainable value. To use a military analogy, you will have allowed the enemy to choose the time and place of battle, increasing the probability that you will be outflanked.

## Business Owners Underestimate the Planning and Effort Required to Successfully Exit

In my experience, most business owners, although they have never sold a business, have bought or sold real estate, possibly on multiple occasions. Hence there is a tendency to assume that the level of complexity in selling a company is roughly comparable, or perhaps slightly more complex, than selling real estate.

Nothing could be further from the truth. Selling a company is exponentially more complex than selling real estate. Information disclosure, for example, is much more complicated, as an investor needs detailed knowledge of the markets in which the company operates, of its business model and its strategy; of how the company generates its revenues, its clients, the technology it uses, and its personnel issues. These are just a few of the additional dimensions that don't exist to nearly the same degree in a real estate transaction. Nor should the human element be underestimated: whereas a real estate transaction usually involves the transfer of bricks and mortar, when you sell a business, the new owners will want to understand the strengths and weaknesses of your staff; their aspirations, whether staff salaries correspond to market rates; what the pension obligations are; what training you have given or is still needed; details of possible non-compete agreements, and on and on. And these are only a few of the many potential areas of additional complexity ...

## There Is Often a Mismatch in Negotiating Strength between Owner/Managers and Professional Investors

Investors, whether strategic or financial, generally purchase or invest in companies on a regular basis, and are therefore usually much more experienced in conducting Transactions than individual business owners. So there is often a fundamental mismatch in experience between the purchaser of a business and the seller. This mismatch is augmented by the fact that owners are typically very emotionally bound to their businesses. Professional investors are much less emotional, and therefore generally have a negotiating advantage.

A seasoned veteran who has negotiated the purchases of a dozen companies will not say to an owner who has never negotiated a Transaction, 'Excuse me, we are not a good negotiating match', and stop the negotiation; rather, he or she will try to negotiate the best possible deal, taking full advantage of the situation, and even if they are getting an unconscionably good deal, they will try to make the owner of the business feel good in the process.

## A FEW WORDS OF ADVICE

As the chapters of this book unfold, we will explore how you, as a business owner, can remedy this imbalance. Once again, it boils down to preparation, and typically also involves inviting a number of qualified experts to join your team.

You may be feeling a little intimidated right now by the tangled maze you will need to navigate to exit your company. It is a formidable maze. Yet millions of business owners have exited successfully. The key things to remember are: start as soon as you can before the exit; find a good internal team and good external advisors to whom you can delegate; learn as much as possible about the subject; and follow the advice outlined in this book one step at a time.

# One

# Business Exit Planning

*Before everything else, getting ready is the secret of success.*
—Henry Ford (1863–1947)
American industrialist

**B**usiness Exit Planning is a new subject; it has only acquired currency as a discipline within the last 10 to 15 years, mostly in North America. Until now, students of Business Exit Planning have mostly been advisors (lawyers, investment bankers, auditors, estate planners, etc.) who have seen the potential for a lucrative area of practice, given the relatively few practitioners of this new subject, and that virtually every business owner could benefit from Business Exit Planning.

I take the view that an informed client is always a better client, and that it is to the benefit of business owners as well as their advisors if business owners are equipped with at least the general principles related to Business Exit Planning. This is the objective of Part I, which is organized according to the following logic:

- Chapter 1 is an introduction. It defines Business Exit Planning, explains why it is necessary, and talks about ways in which a business owner may exit a business.
- Chapter 2 builds on these themes by helping business owners define an endgame.
- Chapter 3 analyzes the numerous exit options available to business owners, and the pros and cons of each option.

- Chapter 4 talks about how business owners can build their internal and advisory teams to better position themselves vis-à-vis investors.
- Chapter 5 deals with how to build a business to create value. Topics range from restructuring to corporate governance and from risk management to concrete actions to enhance value.
- Chapter 6 covers the subjects of building a business plan and valuation of a business.
- Chapter 7 deals with tax and estate planning, as well as creative use of insurance, to facilitate exit planning.
- Chapter 8 wraps up the subject of Business Exit Planning with issues such as timing and communications with other shareholders. It then leads into the subject of **Transaction Management** by anticipating issues such as the types of investors that might be targeted and whether business owners should plan for a competitive process.

There is nothing like preparation to ensure success. As the saying goes, "a goal without a plan is just a wish". Part I is designed to give business owners the tools to create your own road map to a short-term or long-term exit.

# CHAPTER 1

# An Introduction to Business Exit Planning

*I am prepared for the worst, but hope for the best.*
—Benjamin Disraeli (1804–1881)
British statesman

In some languages and cultures, the concept of success is very much associated with exiting. For example, the Spanish word *éxito* means 'success'. The word comes from the Latin verb *exeo*, meaning 'to exit'. Similarly, in Italian, *riuscire* means 'to succeed', whereas the word *uscire* means 'to exit'. There is much logic to this. To enter a war, for example (think of Vietnam, Iraq, and Afghanistan), is the easy part. To exit is much trickier—and you cannot call it a success until you have exited. An investment is similar; making the investment (e.g. buying shares) is the easy part, but you won't know whether you have been successful (i.e. made a profit) until you have sold it. Your company is no different. With the benefit of hindsight, a successful exit from your business is a precondition to your ownership of that business being considered a success. As American financier and investor Henry Kravis stated, "Don't congratulate us when we buy a company. Any fool can buy a company. Congratulate us when we sell it and when we've done something with it and created real value."

> A successful exit from your business is a precondition to your ownership of that business being considered a success.

In this chapter, I will introduce the numerous business exit options that a business owner might explore, and attempt a definition of Business Exit

Planning. I will then provide some statistical evidence further underlining the need for business owners to engage in Business Exit Planning, and finish the chapter with a discussion on the need to understand your own motives with respect to Business Exit Planning and to set clear objectives in any Business Exit Planning exercise.

## WAYS TO EXIT YOUR BUSINESS

Most people associate a **Business Exit** with selling their businesses to third parties, and this is, perhaps, the most common form. But there are many other ways to exit your business:

- *Intergenerational Transfer:* Transfer of ownership to one or more of your children or other relatives.
- *Management Buyout (MBO):* Transfer of ownership to one or more members of your management team.
- *Initial Public Offering (IPO):* Also known as going public, this involves selling shares of your company on a stock exchange. These may be your shares (e.g. funding your exit) or you may have your company issue new shares (e.g. treasury shares), the proceeds of which would flow into your company's bank account, or a combination of the two.
- *Merger:* This involves merging your company with another company to create a new, combined entity. Under the terms of the merger, there may be provisions in the agreement to purchase a portion of your shares at closing, or perhaps all your shares over time.
- *Hiring management:* This option involves hiring professional management to run the business, with the owners withdrawing from day-to-day management of the company. (This is an exit from an operational point of view, but not from an ownership or financial point of view.)
- *Refinancing:* You may be able to extract considerable cash from your business if you find a bank or other financial institution to lend money to your company. (While this may facilitate a partial or considerable exit from a financial viewpoint, it does not achieve any form of exit from an operational point of view.)
- *Employee Share Ownership Plan (ESOP):* This involves selling shares to the employees of your company.
- *Liquidation:* Some businesses are worth more if broken up and liquidated than operated or sold as a going concern.

## WHAT IS BUSINESS EXIT PLANNING?

**Business Exit Planning** is the process of explicitly defining exit-related objectives for the owner(s) of a business, followed by the design of a comprehensive strategy and road map that takes into account all personal, business, financial, legal, and taxation aspects of achieving those objectives, usually in the context of planning the leadership succession and continuity of the business. Objectives may include maximizing (or setting a goal for) proceeds, minimizing risk, closing the sale quickly, or selecting an investor that will ensure that the business prospers (whether because of depth of knowledge or depth of pocket). The strategy will usually include the mode of exit envisaged (IPO, MBO, sale, etc.), a marketing strategy, and a timetable. The strategy should also take into account contingencies such as illness or death.

The Business Exit Planning process typically involves tax planning, as one of your objectives as a business owner will be to maximize *after-tax* proceeds. It may additionally involve estate planning, if your objective is to pass at least part of the proceeds to the next generation.

> It is important for you not only to know your objectives, but also to prioritize them, so as to be in a position to make tradeoffs

It should be understood that some of these objectives may be contradictory. For example, maximizing the speed of a transfer will probably be to the detriment of maximizing proceeds. Hence, it is important for you not only to know your objectives, but also to prioritize them, so as to be in a position to make tradeoffs. Professional judgments may also be involved in making these tradeoffs (e.g. is it worth accelerating the sale process by two months if it is likely to reduce **Transaction** revenues by 30 percent or more?).

As with most things in life, if you do not set your objectives and map out a strategy for achieving them, actually achieving those (undefined!) objectives will be a pure accident. Engaging in Business Exit Planning should increase your chances of a successful business exit. It will help you to:

- maximize the proceeds of the exit;
- minimize taxes, hence maximizing the after-tax proceeds of the exit;
- ensure an orderly transition for the leadership of your company, to a party likely to take the business to the next level;

- define your post-exit activities;
- invest the proceeds of your exit wisely; and
- reduce the level of stress and risk in the Business Exit process.

> Some exit strategies allow you to exit in terms of your personal involvement with the business; some allow you to exit in the financial sense; some allow you to exit in both senses.

As mentioned in the Preface, some exit strategies allow you to exit in terms of your personal involvement with the business; some allow you to exit in the financial sense; some allow you to exit in both senses. I urge you to consider all options to the extent they are appropriate. Weigh all of your options before committing to a course of action. The appropriate exit strategy will depend on your objectives.

## EVIDENCE ON WHY BUSINESS EXIT PLANNING IS NECESSARY

If the example of my father's company has not convinced you of the need for Business Exit Planning, allow me to muster some statistics to support the proposition that it is necessary. A 1996 study of 749 heirs of U.S. family businesses revealed the following:[1]

- In nearly half (47.7 percent) of the cases, the transition and ultimate collapse of the business was precipitated by the founder's death.
- Only in relatively few instances (16.4 percent) did the business failure follow an orderly transition between the owner and the next generation; in situations where the owner was forced to retire, the figure dropped to 6.1 percent.
- Most heirs, regardless of the industry, believed the business failures were the result of inadequate estate/financial planning, poor preparation for the transfer, or a lack of assets to cover the estate taxes. Other reasons given were conflicts with non-active family members and insufficient capital with which to effectively run the business.
- While most owners (76 percent) had estate plans, in the opinions of the heirs, most were severely flawed and did not provide sufficient resources for the business transitions or estate tax obligations.

In the United States, it has been estimated that only 28 percent of private businesses have engaged in any exit planning.[2] According to a 2008 Canadian survey, only one in 20 businesses have a written succession plan.[3] In other parts of the world, this figure is likely to be lower. It is not surprising, then, that owners are typically dissatisfied with the results of their Business Exits. In a survey of 300 former business owners, once again in the United States, 75 percent felt that the sale did not accomplish their personal or financial objectives.[4] According to a UK survey, only 7 percent of businesses offered for sale attract a buyer—partly because they are marketed badly and partly because there is no value in the business.[5] So there is definitely enormous scope for improvement with respect to succession and transfer of business ownership, which underscores the importance of Business Exit Planning.

## UNDERSTAND YOUR MOTIVES

Business Exit Planning can be viewed as the blueprint or strategy for the actual Transaction or exit, just as you commission a blueprint before beginning to build a house. It is most effective if your point of departure occurs when you have an understanding of your own motivations and aspirations. In other words, you must know thyself.

> Understand your real motivations for owning your business and why you are considering selling it.

When I say know thyself, I am suggesting that you look inside yourself to understand your real motivations for owning your business and why you are considering selling it. For some owners, owning a business is about drawing an income rather than building equity value in their businesses. For others, it's about supporting a lifestyle with cars, travel, or other perks. Some don't even realize the full extent of wealth generation potential in building equity value. Building equity value is a necessary motivation if you are to build real value in your business, irrespective of whether you are planning to exit. Knowing your real motivations will help you choose the appropriate form, timing, and strategy for exit.

There are a number of possible motivations for exit:

- *Retirement:* You may feel the need to move on to a different phase of your life, enjoy it more, spend more time with your family, relax, and so on. One of my clients, who was outraged whenever anyone mentioned the idea of his retiring or selling, went to the Red Sea on vacation. The vacation was so marvelous that he came back transformed, having realized that there was more to life than running his business. He is now contemplating an eventual exit.

- *Diminished passion or energy:* It is unlikely that your business will be successful unless you have the energy and passion to make it a success. If you lack either, it is probably better to exit sooner rather than later. If you are suffering from burnout, try an extended holiday. A surprising number of business owners are simply bored by the monotony of running a business, and feel they need to escape in order to pursue self-actualization or bring more balance to their lives.

- *Your current or expected state of health:* If you are in your 50s, 60s or 70s, what kind of condition is your body in? What are your health risks? If you have less energy now than you had, say, three to five years ago, there is a good chance that you will have even less, three to five years from now. Will that leave you with sufficient vigor and energy to run your business? Have you been diagnosed with a condition that is likely to deteriorate over time?

- *Lack of capital:* Every business needs capital to grow. If you started a business in a very capital-intensive industry, there is a high probability that you may run into limits to growth and may require funding (see Box 1.1). There are many high-tech companies that develop an exciting product and then lack capital to take it to global markets. For such companies, a sale may produce far more shareholder wealth than an underfunded expansion, and the product will likely receive a much better launch.

- *Dispute resolution:* A Business Exit is sometimes triggered by various forms of dispute; for example, a divorce may force the sale of a business, or you may be at odds with your co-shareholder. Sometimes the sale of a business is just the cleanest, easiest way to solve the dispute. There may be a lack of liquidity to satisfy the other party or parties unless the business is sold.

- *Increase in risk:* When the regulations or legislation governing an industry change, the regulatory risk of your business may increase. For example, there may be less flexibility on raising prices, more difficulty in passing through costs, or a higher risk of penalties. An increase in competitive forces may also increase risk levels. For whatever reason, your business might just be getting too risky, or as you advance in years, your appetite for risk may diminish.

- *Portfolio diversification:* Some wealth planners suggest that no one should have more than 20 percent of their net worth tied up in any

---

### BOX 1.1    ENERGY SERVICES COMPANY

The owner of an energy services company (ESCO) had developed an extremely interesting business model, whereby it replaced the archaic heating equipment of old public buildings (hospitals, prisons, municipal buildings, etc.) with brand new, energy-efficient heating equipment. This cost on average between €250,000 and €1 million per installation.

ESCO designed, installed, and maintained the equipment during a long-term contract (typically 10 to 15 years). The energy savings were more than enough to provide the company with a handsome return on capital, as well as to reduce the energy costs of the public authority. The business was very profitable.

So why did the owner sell? Growth of this type of company is extremely capital intensive. He had reached his capital limit. The banks had indicated that they would be unwilling to keep up with the growth of the company without an equity injection, so either massive amounts of fresh equity would be required, or a much stronger covenant would be needed to guarantee the loan.

In a nutshell, ESCO was worth a great deal more to an investor with deep pockets, who could take advantage of all the opportunities available to the company. The company was sold to a global corporation that was able to not only better finance the growth opportunities, but also to utilize further opportunities to leverage the particular expertise of ESCO globally.

---

single investment. While we can argue about the correct percentage, many business owners (my father included) exceed any kind of prudent share of net worth tied up in their businesses. Generally, portfolio and risk diversification becomes even more important with age, as retirement approaches.

> Many business owners exceed any kind of prudent share of net worth tied up in their businesses

Investors will want to know your reasons or motivations for selling your business, and are likely to ask the question directly. You should have an appropriate answer prepared. Retirement, for example, is considered an excellent reason by most investors. But if you wait too long to sell your business, and develop medical problems that prevent you from working full-time with energy and passion, most investors will sense it. Postpone beyond a certain point, and it inevitably becomes a distress sale. As was the case with my father, if the owner faces an urgent exit, or might not be available to assist with an orderly transition, the valuation is likely to be negatively impacted, or investor interest may fail to materialize altogether.

As a business owner, you should constantly be assessing the cost/benefit analysis of retaining ownership of your company versus selling it. There are potential benefits to retaining the business if it is possible to grow the value of the company in the near future. But there are also risks: a recession may diminish the value of your business; competition may intensify; some of your key staff may leave; your own health may unexpectedly deteriorate; or someone may commence litigation against your company.

## THE SPECIAL CASE OF RETIREMENT

For a business owner, retirement can be like going from full speed to full stop literally overnight. Some business owners get cold feet when they are selling their businesses and withdraw from or even sabotage a Transaction because they cannot come to terms with the concept of retirement. Some business owners, consciously or subconsciously, harbor deep-seated fears about retirement, as if it were an admission of giving up, of having one foot in the grave. And yet there are also countless examples of owners who retire early, develop new meaning for living, re-invent themselves, and continue to lead extremely active and productive lives. As the saying goes: perception is reality. The old notion that retirement is essentially inactivity or a vacation is no longer applicable. Many retirees are very active at least into their 70s, consulting, enjoying a second source of income, contributing their time to charity, etc.

Problems may arise in cases where owners have pursued their businesses with such singular focus that they have neglected other interests, and so have trouble contemplating any transition. If you are one of these owners, the 'know thyself' principle is all the more important: you need to develop activities that can be pursued outside of work. Children or grandchildren? Consulting? A few Board positions? Social activities? Travel? Or like Bill Gates, you can spend the first phase of your life making money, and the next phase of your life giving it away. There are many activities and opportunities you can pursue once you've sold your business.

Experts talk about the 'addiction' of owners to their businesses. Apparently business owners fear that after retirement their "bodies will not be fed the necessary dose of chemicals required from the business addiction."[6] It sounds very much like athletes addicted to their sport: intense physical activity may release morphine-type stimulants known as endorphins. There is much to be potentially addicted to when running a business: power, lifestyle, expense accounts, travel, and the perks of owning a company, not to mention the stimulation from negotiations, meetings, and teamwork. You should understand the possibility of such an addiction for a couple of reasons. First, because it might interfere with rational thinking (e.g. a business owner might be ageing and infirm, and refuse to contemplate exit because of his/her addiction); and second, because there are a surprising number of business owners who get as far as negotiating a **Sale and Purchase Agreement** (SPA) and then, suddenly realizing that they are incapable of shaking their addiction, back out of the deal.

Planning future activities can help prevent or minimize that feeling of going from full speed to full stop. Write that book. Seek out a few board positions. Plan that around-the-world trip. Reactivate some of your old hobbies. Start a new one. Take up golf. Start playing a musical instrument. Attend Rotary meetings. Whatever it takes. Find something that will motivate you, something that you will enjoy. You have multiple facets to your personality, and life beyond your business is your chance to explore these. Plan ahead.

> Relatively few business owners miss their businesses once they've sold them.

Surprisingly, relatively few business owners miss their businesses once they've sold them. A 2006 UK survey showed that only 8 percent of former owners of family-owned businesses missed their businesses and only 18 percent would ever consider getting back into the business.[7]

Whereas a century ago, average life expectancy barely exceeded retirement age (for those fortunate enough to reach retirement), today, the average individual in most developed economies may expect to have one or more decades of retirement. With advances in medicine, the time we spend in retirement is likely to increase even further. So, the importance of planning for retirement cannot be underestimated.

If you are like most business owners, you probably see the sale of your business funding your retirement. A 2004 Australian survey, for example, noted that 50 percent of business owners expected the sale of their businesses to fund their retirement.[8]

# CHAPTER 2

# Begin with the Endgame in Sight

*If you don't know where you are going, every road will get you nowhere.*

—Henry Kissinger (b. 1923)
American political scientist

Is your business in day-to-day survival mode, or are you working toward a vision of what you are trying to create by the time you exit? Businesses that are in day-to-day survival mode are generally unsaleable or have very little value.

Other businesses operate at a level considerably better than survival mode, and may even have solid cash flow and good profits, but their main objective seems to be creating an annuity for the owner or providing a foundation for his or her lifestyle (these are sometimes referred to as *lifestyle businesses*), rather than investing the necessary funds in research and development, marketing, or other investments necessary to maximize opportunity and value. The owner or management might be satisfied with the business in its current state, but such businesses will likely see their competitive advantage eroded before too long.

Many investors like to see big, hairy, ambitious goals where the company has already made considerable progress toward achieving them. Investors will pay a premium if they detect that the company has clear goals based on excellent growth prospects and that the management has genuine ambition, as well as an established track record in achieving them.

Investors don't like to see businesses following a strategy of siphoning off profits so as to minimize taxes. This destroys shareholder value. Some business owners offer convoluted explanations as to how these siphoned (and often untraceable funds) should nevertheless contribute to the value of the company, because ultimately it is the potential to generate earnings that counts toward valuation, but the majority of investors won't buy that logic. They will likely be very concerned with the potential liabilities that such actions may bring to the company.

This chapter deals with developing that game plan for where you want to take your business before exit. It's a game plan that should motivate you, but also one that will motivate others to invest in your business.

> If you want to maximize your exit proceeds, you need to develop a game plan that takes advantage of a major market opportunity, and every day move closer to realizing it

## DEVELOP A GAME PLAN

If you want to maximize your exit proceeds, you need to develop a game plan that takes advantage of a major market opportunity, and every day move closer to realizing it (see Box 2.1). Elements of a game plan should include:

- *Strategy:* Your strategy is like the blueprint for building a house. What markets do you propose to serve, and with what products or services? What is your business model? How do you generate revenue and

---

### BOX 2.1　MARKETING CONSULTING COMPANY

The owner of a marketing consulting company had a clear vision: he wanted to sell his company in five years for €25 million. He passionately identified with this goal, but knew neither what his business was worth at the time, nor whether the goal was realistic or achievable.

We conducted a **Business Exit Planning** exercise whereby the current value of his business was established at approximately €7 million. We then established a set of targets and benchmarks year by year, which brought the business to €25 million in value at the end of five years. The owner was pleased because now he could use these benchmarks to motivate the members of his management team and have them buy into the vision, along with tying stock options to achieving the benchmarks.

value? What is the potential for growth? What is your unique selling proposition (USP)? How do you differentiate yourself from the competition? What systems, resources, and implementation plans do you have to achieve your strategy?

- *Business Plan:* Have you forecasted cash flow and profit/loss? Most investors will expect the next 12 to 24 months to be broken down by month, and the breakdown for up to the next five years to be on an annual basis.

- *Time Period:* You may want to take several years to enhance the value of your business before selling it; it may also take a year or two to actually sell it (especially if it is not successfully sold on the first attempt). The new owners will quite possibly ask you to participate in an orderly transition, potentially lasting several more years.

- *Put it in Writing:* Putting your strategy and Business Plan into writing should be of considerable value to you as a business owner; investors will also want to see these documents. They demonstrate a direction and a sense of purpose. There is something about putting things in writing that sharpens the mind, creates focus, and helps banish fuzzy thinking. Obviously, the quality of thinking that goes into the strategy and Business Plan will determine their ultimate success, along with how persuasive they are for investors. While the writing of a strategy or Business Plan is beyond the scope of this book, you need to recognize their importance; there are numerous courses and books on the subject.

> Having your eye on long-term goals can help overcome short-term setbacks.

## VALUE SYSTEMS AND VISUALIZING THE ENDGAME

When I say visualize the endgame, I mean that, like a good athlete who envisions the competition ahead, you should visualize the look and feel of your business when it has achieved success and fulfilled your plans. This anchor to the future will help draw you forward. And as John Lennon once said: life is what happens to you while you're busy making other plans. Having your eye on long-term goals can help overcome short-term setbacks. Private equity groups, for example, will typically not invest in a business unless they already have an exit strategy in sight. They are applying the principle of visualizing the endgame.

Ultimately, how anyone visualizes the endgame is a function of that person's value system. Ideally, the endgame visualized should be one that motivates both the business owner as well as potential investors. It is of great assistance to business owners if you have someone you can rely on to give you an objective assessment as to whether the endgame you visualized will also motivate outside investors. A frequent challenge for business owners is the need to develop clarity not only on your own values and vision of endgame, and that of investors, but for all major stakeholders, such as your family, your management team, and your co-shareholders, all of which are very different, and often contradict each other:

- Family values are usually based on unconditional love, emotion, support, acceptance, and child development.
- Management values are to generate profit, increase wealth, improve the business, and reduce risk. These values are typically rational and analytical. Acceptance and reward are typically conditional on performance.
- Shareholders are typically focused primarily on wealth creation and balancing risks.

Table 2.1 summarizes these three value systems.

Notice the great potential for conflict among the three value systems. If you are a business owner, the CEO of your business, and the head of a family, you must ensure that all stakeholders, who have different value systems, are looked after. One of your greatest challenges will be to create alignment in values and vision of endgame between stakeholders. You will need to consider any one course of action from all three perspectives, plus the likely effect on outside investors. This adds to the complexity of Business Exit Planning; sometimes procrastination sets in because the exercise is just too complex, or because it seems impossible to satisfy all stakeholders.

**TABLE 2.1**  Differing Value Systems of Business Stakeholders[1]

| Family | Management | Shareholders |
| --- | --- | --- |
| Needs-based | Performance-based | Finance-based |
| Unconditional loyalty | Conditional loyalty | Return on investment |
| Equality | Unequal | Risk management |
| Cooperation | Competition | Control |
| Wealth consumption | Wealth management | Wealth creation |

If your business is put up for sale a second or third time, or if it has been on the market for a long time, investors may begin to look at it with a jaundiced eye.

Too many business owners just put up their businesses for sale, without adequately considering other exit options. They find out after they have received several offers that their businesses were worth considerably less than what they had expected, or that the profile of their businesses did not match what investors were looking for. Other surprises, such as contingent liabilities, may have derailed the sale process. They could have spared themselves and their management team a great deal of effort, possibly significant advisory fees, and the information getting out on the market that the business was for sale. If your business is put up for sale a second or third time, or if it has been on the market for a long time, investors may begin to look at it with a jaundiced eye. Doing the necessary up-front planning, considering all of your options, greatly increases the chances of getting it right the first time, when you do go to market.

CHAPTER **3**

# Exit Options

*Don't simply retire from something; have something to retire to.*
—H.E. Fosdick (1878–1969)
American clergyman

In Chapter 1, I outlined a number of options to consider other than selling your business. While each of these could be the subject of a book themselves, in this chapter I intend to summarize what, in my experience, business owners have found to be the pros and cons of each option. Let's start with the pros and cons of each option *other than* a conventional sale; then, look at the pros and cons of a conventional sale, and possible variations.

## INTERGENERATIONAL TRANSFER

An **Intergenerational Transfer** is the transfer of ownership to one or more children or relatives. Some of the factors that might contribute to you considering an Intergenerational Transfer include:

- If you have one or more heirs apparent who have a demonstrated aptitude and desire for running the business.
- If the business itself is a good investment over the long term, and if the family might be hard pressed to find better investments.
- If there are strong family values related to ownership of the family business, and perhaps already a tradition of the company having passed through a number of generations (see Box 3.1).

Most owners of mid-sized companies that I have known who have contemplated Intergenerational Transfers have decided against them, for the following reasons:

## BOX 3.1   CODORNIU, A SPARKLING WINE PRODUCER (SPAIN)

The Spanish company Codorniu is a spectacular example of an Intergenerational Transfer. The company can trace its roots back to at least 1551 and has passed through 17 generations of ownership within the same family. It had revenue of approximately €236 million for the year ending June 2009, and approximately 900 staff.

Codorniu is run by a 12-member Board of Directors, 10 of which are family members (two members from each of the five branches of the family). The President and Chairman of the Board and the General Manager are also family members. The President/Chairman is always selected from the Board.

A Family Code regulates the rules of engagement for family members in the company. For example, family members hired into the company (typically into mid-management functions) must have a university degree, fluency in a second language, and five years of relevant work experience in another firm. Their hiring must also be evaluated by an outside HR consultant and they are never promised promotion.

For the first 14 generations, ownership passed to the eldest son or daughter; since the fifteenth generation, all children have been eligible to inherit. Ownership is now fairly spread out over a wide base of shareholders within the family, with no dominant or controlling vote held by any member or even branch of the family.

There is no particular event that triggers a transfer from one generation to the next. It can be during the life of the shareholder, or upon death. The Board of Directors retains an independent advisor who provides a valuation of the shares in the company, which forms the basis for transfer of value. Where a share is offered to a third party (e.g., a non-family member), family members have the first right of refusal. To date, there has never been a transfer of shares outside the family.

- *Valuations may be lower:* An Intergenerational Transfer may well result in a considerably lower valuation than a competitive sale process.
- *Payment of sale price may be deferred:* The next generation usually doesn't have the cash necessary to pay the market value of the business. Banks may not be willing to finance the purchase price (especially if the next generation does not have a long track record in management), so owners must generally accept payment of the purchase price over time.

- *Timing issues:* Will you as owner be able to run the business with energy and dynamism until the next generation is ready to take over? When my 17-year-old son (my only child) expressed enthusiasm about taking over my corporate finance business, I said to him: "Ok, let's see how this would work out as far as timing. You have four more years of high school, followed by about six years of university (undergraduate and MBA), followed by eight to ten years of work experience. That means you could be ready to take over the business in about 20 years' time. A lot of uncertainty there! Will you still want to take over the business in 20 years? Will I be well enough to run the business for the next 20 years?" In my case, an intergenerational transfer would be a very long-term strategy indeed. And a somewhat risky strategy as well: unless there was some back-up plan, the likelihood of my being in good enough health to manage a grueling business into my seventies is certainly not 100 percent. One should think through the timing issues very carefully.
- *Risk is higher:* There are multiple kinds of risk: risk that the next generation will not manage the business as well as the former owner, in which case there is a risk of the business failing or doing poorly, as well as risk that the next generation will default on its payment obligations to the former owner, triggered by poor performance.

Many owners have been in the business for so long that they are oblivious to the competencies they have acquired over the years, as well as the vast amount of information they have assimilated. Don't underestimate the different competencies required to run your business, from technical skills to softer interpersonal skills, like managing staff or salesmanship.

Much depends on the management and leadership abilities of the next generation. Are you completely objective in assessing your own offspring and their business acumen? This particular adjective—objective—is hardly the first word that comes to mind when assessing how parents think of their children. Some look at their children through rose-tinted glasses, thinking that they can do no wrong; others underestimate their children, thinking they are useless or incapable. Proven track record is always more convincing than theoretical capabilities!

You may wish to consult trusted third parties. There are psychologists who have developed practices in the area of assisting with Intergenerational Transfers. The psychologist with whom I work cannot predict the probability that a child will succeed in following in a parent's footsteps; but he can predict, with close to 100 percent accuracy, when a child is likely to *not* be successful. This is invaluable information that helps avoid setting a child up for failure.

> Having the same genes is no guarantee of success!

According to author and financial advisor Doug Robbins, Intergenerational Transfers fail to meet expectations of the participants nearly 80 percent of the time.[1] Having the same genes is no guarantee of success! Nevertheless, there are some spectacular successes (see Box 3.1). Northern Italy and Germany's *mittelstand** companies are well known for Intergenerational Transfers.

One way of managing the risk associated with an Intergenerational Transfer in a borderline case might be rotating the next generation through various positions in the firm, and, if successful, delegating the CEO function for a time before transferring ownership. The transfer of ownership might then be gradual. Be sensitive to the issues that may be created by fast-tracking your own offspring at the expense of other staff in your company.

*Taking over a business from a successful (and often domineering) parent is an intensely personal affair, not an easy task. Family politics or intergenerational issues may also create enormous difficulties. A successful transfer requires as much effort from the parent as from the next generation (and sometimes restraint!)*

Generally, only a subset of mid-sized companies can seriously consider this as an optimal exit strategy.

## INITIAL PUBLIC OFFERING

Almost every business owner dreams of hitting the jackpot by going public on a stock exchange. Yet when many owners find out what is involved in taking their company public, they recoil in horror, rapidly coming to the conclusion that this is not for them.

### The case for going public
- Raising equity at favorable valuations: An **Initial Public Offering** (IPO) may allow shareholders to raise substantial fresh equity at extremely

---

*German medium-sized enterprises.

favorable valuations. This may be used to fund the exit of one or more existing shareholders, or to raise fresh equity for the company. If the timing is right, when market conditions are good, the equity raised may be extremely cheap. For example, on the Warsaw Stock Exchange at the peak of the market in 2007, stocks of mid-sized companies traded at over 25 times EBITDA (Earnings Before Income, Tax, Depreciation, and Amortization). At the time, this was approximately three to four times the value that most private equity firms or strategic investors would have been prepared to pay for comparable firms.

- Creating a currency for acquisitions or compensation: If your company has an aggressive acquisition program, it may use its own shares to fund acquisitions, rather than cash. Similarly, it may offer shares rather than cash to management or other staff, in lieu of bonuses. This will allow the company to conserve cash and may motivate management (or shareholders in the acquired company) to work hard in order to further improve share prices.

- Ongoing access to equity capital: Where a company has a public listing, it may return to the capital markets relatively easily for additional capital, provided that market conditions and perception of the company are favorable.

- Prestige: A successful public listing may contribute to a positive public perception and image of the company, perhaps even building brand loyalty.

### The case against going public

- Costs and risks of going public: Taking a medium-sized company public can easily cost hundreds of thousands, possibly even millions; these costs may consume 10 to 15 percent or more of the proceeds. The company must fund a significant portion of these costs prior to the IPO. If market conditions change and the IPO fails, the company will still be saddled with considerable expense. Despite the fact that the majority of costs are usually success related, there are still likely to be considerable fixed costs (e.g., legal fees).

- Reputational risk: The risk of such a public failure concerns some business owners, not just in terms of the money involved but also because of the possible negative publicity. A number of companies have gone bankrupt when their reputations suffered from a failed IPO.

- Short-term pressures: Expectations of public companies are very focused on quarterly earnings. If your business is highly cyclical, or requires long-term thinking, an IPO may be a recipe for disaster.

▪ Costs of ongoing information provision and compliance: A public company must be fully transparent. At the time of going public, a prospectus or offering memorandum must provide full disclosure of all the information relevant to potential investors assessing the company. After going public, the company must generally file quarterly statements intended to update the shareholding public with respect to all material developments concerning the company, as well as special filings when these material developments occur. Collecting and disseminating this information has a cost, in terms of the staff-time required to collect the information and to prepare the reports. Giving your competitors detailed information on your operations may have a less quantifiable but potentially very damaging cost. Also, there are various costs related to compliance: stock exchanges will generally require public companies to have a Board of Directors (which will in turn ask for liability insurance) and various committees of the Board (e.g., Audit Committee, Compensation Committee); the costs involved in these can be significant.

▪ Costs of shareholder communications and public relations: Once a company goes public, it must maintain ongoing communications with shareholders and the general public. Will analysts follow the stock and regularly report on the company's activities? This is a necessary precondition for achieving the confidence of investors and is generally only worthwhile for analysts once a company's market capitalization reaches a certain scale (often in the hundreds of millions). If such a following in the analyst community fails to develop, the general public will not receive the information and independent verification that it requires in order to develop the confidence necessary to invest in the company's shares. This can cause the share price to languish far below the price at which the company initially went public, also far below the real worth of the company. This in turn may make it more difficult to raise additional financing or to engage in mergers and acquisitions, as investors will tend to use the market capitalization of the company as a proxy for its value.

▪ Possible liabilities: A company that does not provide full disclosure (e.g., where there is an error, omission, or delay in the provision of information) may face potential liabilities. Class actions by shareholders are common in the United States and in other jurisdictions.

▪ New skill sets and corporate culture: Going public often requires new skill sets and corporate culture. More emphasis on reporting may reduce entrepreneurialism. The corporate culture may need to change to one of greater transparency, or to a more short-term way of thinking (e.g., meeting targets for the next quarter).

- The possibility of hostile takeover: Once you sell more than 50 percent of the shares in your company, you may wake up one morning to face the risk of losing control of it in the event of a hostile takeover bid.
- Not really an exit: Going public solves the issue of raising capital, but it doesn't solve the issue of succession. Chances are that if you go public, you will have a considerable portion of your net worth locked up (many stock exchanges prescribe lock up periods of up to several years, during which period pre-IPO shareholders may not sell shares). You may also find it hard to extricate yourself from the day-to-day running of the business.

Generally, a compelling growth story is a necessary prerequisite for a successful IPO. Going public is a decision that requires careful consideration.

Most companies that are in a position to go public have a choice of a number of stock exchanges. It is important to consider the pros and cons of each exchange; most importantly, which exchange is best suited to attracting investors for your company. Those that are more prestigious and have greater liquidity, for example, are generally more expensive and have more stringent reporting requirements.

An IPO is not for every company. Once again, only a small subset of mid-sized, privately owned companies are serious candidates for IPOs. For those companies, it may be a truly excellent option.

## MERGER

Another option for exit, which once again might be appropriate for a small subset of companies, is a merger. The pros and cons of a merger are not as black and white as for an IPO. Much depends on the details of what is negotiated, and its implementation.

A merger occurs when two or more companies combine to form a new, larger, merged entity, usually resulting in synergies (e.g., stronger market position, economies of scale on procurement or other operating costs). It is the synergies that usually provide the motivation for a merger, although sometimes the motivation may be to allow an owner or manager to exit, or even to generate cash for the party that exits. The terms of the merger will determine how much equity, cash, or debt you take by way of compensation, as well as the locus of control. It is not easy to find a merger partner that is appropriate for your company, where you can negotiate merger terms and conditions that satisfy your objectives.

> At some point, a merger may begin to resemble an outright sale.

The term merger may give the impression of a partnership of equals, and negotiations may begin in such a fashion. But in most mergers that I have seen, the shareholders of one of the merging entities end up taking control of the merged entity, leaving only minority rights for the other entity. At some point, a merger may begin to resemble an outright sale.

If you are considering the option of exit via merger, you should either be prepared to take control of a merged entity and create the synergies, or become a more passive player in an organization controlled by other shareholders. In the latter event, the successful exit from your shareholding may depend on the business acumen of the controlling shareholders. You should assess, from your knowledge of them, whether you would be prepared to take this risk. You may also wish to negotiate a **Buy-Sell Agreement** or a **Put Option** with the majority shareholder(s), because exiting from a minority position can be much more challenging than exiting from a majority position.

A merger is an option that might be explored where there is no buyer on the horizon who is willing to pay cash. In times of economic recession, for example, it may provide a way for the owners of two marginal or loss-making companies to combine forces and, through synergies or economies of scale, create one stronger enterprise with a valuation greater than the sum of the parts. A successful merger may create an entity with sufficient critical mass to be a desirable target for an investor.

A merger, in and of itself, does not assure any of the owners of the merging companies that they will be able to retire or withdraw from active management. This will depend on the terms of the merger.

## HIRING PROFESSIONAL MANAGEMENT

Some business owners exit the operational running of their companies by hiring professional management, focusing instead on overseeing the company in the capacity of shareholder and Board member. In this type of arrangement, it is important to bear in mind that virtually all business risk will remain with you, as the business owner, in your capacity as shareholder. Will the professional managers be as good and as conscientious about running the business as you were? This is a significant business risk.

Most business owners try to create this motivation by offering generous performance-related bonuses to the professional management. If the business goes well, there should be enough to share with the professional managers and keep them motivated. If the business sustains losses, however, it may be difficult to retain and motivate professional managers without these performance-related bonuses.

Achieving a real alignment between the interests of professional managers and shareholders is a challenge. For example, you might pay managers bonuses or stock options based on performance (e.g., financial results). But what about the level of risk assumed to boost the performance? That is much harder to factor into the equation. Remember the recent cases of heads of Wall Street financial firms taking huge speculative risks with shareholder funds and then drawing substantial bonuses?

Having a professional manager who also has an ownership interest in your company helps to create a better alignment of interests with shareholders; the more shares the professional manager acquires, the better the alignment begins to look. But it's also the case that the more shares you transfer, the more the activity begins to resemble a sale of your business.

## MANAGEMENT BUYOUT

A **Management Buyout** (**MBO**) should only be considered where management has the necessary aptitude to run the business and a strong desire to take control. Having a serious, motivated, and competent management team is key to the success of your business, and should be recognized. Many owners think of management as extended family, and all else being equal, would rather sell to those who have helped create the wealth than to an independent, possibly hitherto unknown, third party.

In the event that you consider an MBO, you will need to decide whether you want to negotiate with management separately, or whether you will allow managers to participate on an equal footing in a fully competitive sale process. If you decide to negotiate separately, the valuation will seldom be comparable to that achieved in a fully competitive process. Managers are often cash poor and must usually seek debt or equity financing from private equity firms, banks, or other sources, which may add delays and uncertainty to a **Transaction**. Alternatively, they may seek special terms, such as **Vendor Financing** in the form of deferred payments for shares.

When managers purchase your business, there is also the potential for moral hazard.

When managers purchase your business, there is also the potential for moral hazard. For example, if, in the months prior to closing, the performance of the business goes down, assuming valuation of the MBO is tied to performance, you can never be 100 percent sure whether your managers really did their best to enhance the performance (and hence the value) of your business. Or if your management team is participating in a competitive process as one of several bidders, you can never be fully sure whether the independent bidders had quite the same access to information (e.g., that there is a lucrative contract that is likely to be signed in several months).

An MBO may be a large leap for a management team. Will your managers, who have been operating as subordinates, be able to morph into leaders in their own right? Do they have the entrepreneurial talent required? You, as their leader, are probably best placed to answer such questions. Once again, firms that are candidates for an MBO form a small percentage of mid-sized firms.

A word of caution: As the business owner, you should be careful about initiating discussions with management about an MBO, if, for example, you are considering it as one of your options. Bringing up the subject may raise expectations, and if you are ultimately unable to deliver, you may end up with a demotivated management team. Be careful of raising expectations.

## REFINANCING

Obtaining a loan, mezzanine, preferred shares, or other form of financing for your company may be one way of fulfilling at least a partial exit, from a financial point of view.[†] To the extent that you own a limited liability corporation, and the lender's cash is substituting for the cash that you, as an owner, withdraw from the business, you are de facto transferring your risk as the owner to the lender. Of course, this transference of risk does not occur if you provide the bank or financial institution with a personal guarantee.

Private equity firms are masters at refinancing. With strong banking ties, they are sometimes able to convince banks to leverage their companies to the hilt, and pull out all of the cash they have invested into the business—sometimes even more. This allows them to report a fantastic return on equity.

---

[†]Mezzanine and preferred shares are known as 'hybrids' between debt and equity that have features of each.

Before you decide on this option, consider the downsides of high leverage. Financial institutions, even if they don't require a guarantee, will likely require various covenants, such as operating income covering interest expense by a comfortable margin. Failure to do so will trigger a default. Are you and your business prepared to take this degree of risk?

## EMPLOYEE STOCK OWNERSHIP PLAN

This option generally suits those types of owners who wish to take some money off the table, so that they may financially diversify their portfolios, while still keeping control of their businesses. There's little point in going into more detail here, as **Employee Stock Ownership Plan (ESOP)** regimes are very country specific. Some countries have specific legislation to encourage share ownership by employees. This legislation may allow shareholders to defer or to be exempt from certain taxes.

## LIQUIDATION

According to a 2004 Australian study, 17 percent of business owners plan to liquidate their businesses when the time comes to exit.[2] This may be because they realize that the business is not saleable, or because the business has little or no value.

But liquidation may also present opportunities. If you own a factory, a golf course, or a plant nursery, for example, which has been overtaken by urban growth, the real estate itself may be worth considerably more than the business is as a going concern. Sometimes the individual parts are worth more than the whole. In such cases, liquidation may unlock value.

If you own a profitable business though, it is likely to be worth more as a going concern and should be sold as such, rather than liquidated. Liquidation, in such cases, should be a last resort; something you do only if you are unable to exit and cannot find a successor, or if your business is worth more when broken up.

## CHOOSING THE RIGHT EXIT OPTION

If you believe that you have more options than you really do with respect to a Business Exit, you're not alone. Many business owners think this. If you examine each of the options, whether IPO, Intergenerational Transfer, MBO, or merger, it will become apparent that not all options will suit your

particular situation. That is not to say they should not be considered seriously. If you're like the majority of owners of mid-sized businesses, however,
it will generally be the sale of your business that will constitute the exit
option best suited to fulfilling your objectives, assuming that those objectives call for achieving a satisfactory purchase price and liquidity, and that
you have created real equity value in your business.

So, while the remainder of this book is written from the perspective of
selling your business, much of it will still apply to other forms of transfer,
as in the following cases:

- If you think that you will need to provide a great deal of information
  to potential investors under the **Due Diligence** process, you will need
  to provide at least as much information if you perform an IPO.
- While the Due Diligence required in an Intergenerational Transfer or
  MBO may not be as extensive, there will still be issues of valuation and
  deal structuring.
- With respect to a merger, in all likelihood a relative valuation of both
  entities will be required, as well as a reciprocal Due Diligence, where
  each merging partner performs Due Diligence of the other.

Nevertheless, the vast majority of Business Exits will involve some kind
of Transaction; so even though I'll spend the remainder of the book focusing
on a Transaction of a 'business sale' variety, much of what I have to say
will still be applicable to other forms of Transactions.

The option of selling your business does not have just one simple
variant of selling 100 percent of the equity of your business on closing; it
also has variations on a theme:

- *Sale of a minority interest in your business:* You might sell only 10,
  20, or 30 percent of your business in the first instance. This might allow
  you to cement a strategic alliance with an important partner who may
  provide synergies. Depending on the terms of your agreement, the
  investor might have the obligation or the option to buy you out should
  certain predefined events occur, such as death or incapacity. This may
  be an important first step to ensuring that your business survives you.
- *Sale of a majority interest in your business:* This makes sense where
  you want to take a bigger step back from owning and running your
  business or have the risk of majority ownership pass to a third party.
  Compared to the option of selling a minority interest, the sale of a
  majority interest allows you to reap a **Control Premium**; for example,
  a higher price per share that is associated with the right to direct the
  affairs of the company.

- *Private equity recapitalization:* This involves a private equity firm buying control of your company, plus providing a capital infusion, leaving you, the owner, with a minority stake (usually in the range 15 to 20 percent). As the owner, you will enter into a contract to continue running the company, and will stay on until the exit of the private equity fund, with the potential to earn more on the sale of your 15 to 20 percent stake than on the initial majority sale (see Box 3.2).

> The trick is to find the option that best fits your objectives and is acceptable to an investor.

Even under the first two options, when you are selling only part of your business, you should spare a thought for whether you wish the proceeds from the sale to flow into your shareholders' bank accounts (e.g., when shareholders sell their shares). Alternatively, all or a portion of the proceeds may flow into the company's bank account (e.g., when new shares in the company are sold). In other words, a sale of shares may be used as a way to capitalize the company or to fund the exit of one or more existing shareholders, or a combination of capitalization and exit. Either of the minority or majority sale options may be accompanied by an **Earn-Out**, where the

---

### BOX 3.2    PRIVATE EQUITY RECAPITALIZATION

In the late 1990s, as CEO of a telecommunications company, I was negotiating the purchase of an Internet Service Provider (ISP). We had reached a fairly advanced stage of negotiation, and had agreed on a purchase price of $7 million for 100 percent of the equity.

Then, for some reason, the party representing the vendor did not return my calls for several weeks. Finally, when we met, he told me that we had no deal. He had reached agreement with another investor, a private equity investor, who had purchased 35 percent of the company for approximately $3 million. The majority of this money was to purchase shares newly issued by the company, by way of cash injection.

Less than three years later, the company was sold for $33 million. Such is the potential power of equity recapitalization combined with a growth opportunity.

investor buys out your remaining shares according to a pre-defined formula over a pre-defined period of time.

As you can see, there are almost an infinite number of options in planning this chess game of Business Exit. The trick is to find the option that best fits your objectives and is acceptable to an investor. Whether your objective is to exit financially, or to phase out your own personal involvement, or both, you'll need some creative deal structuring. Defining and communicating your objectives at the outset of any planning process is the first step to successful realization.

# CHAPTER 4

# Building Your Team to Assist Your Exit

*I want people who will stand up to me. People who are not afraid to say exactly what's on their minds, even though that's probably not what I want to hear. That's what I want.*
— Henry Kravis (b. 1944)
American business financier and investor

The sale of a business almost always involves building a team that will need to work cooperatively to plan and execute your exit. Remember the fundamental mismatch in negotiating strength between professional investors, who have purchased numerous companies, and owners/managers, who have seldom (if ever) sold a company! Building your team helps reduce or eliminates this mismatch in negotiating strength.

In this chapter, I will discuss in more detail the reasons for building a team, composition and role of your advisory team, and ethical considerations in assembling your team.

## REASONS FOR BUILDING A TEAM

There are several reasons for considering building a team:

- *Multidisciplinary effort:* If you are seriously considering **Business Exit Planning** and an eventual exit, you need to build a multidisciplinary team, consisting of internal staff and, to the extent necessary, external advisors. Your team will typically need to include expertise in the areas of law, corporate finance, accounting, taxation, and possibly also in certain technical, environmental, or other subjects, to name but a few.

The chances that you, as the owner/manager of a mid-sized business, have all this expertise in-house are quite slim. Missing just one may be damaging or even fatal to the success of your exit.

- *Adversarial process:* Although sellers and buyers of businesses may get along very well, be aware that the situation and the process are—by definition—adversarial. Just to provide two examples:
  - The investor wants to buy at the lowest possible price, while you as the owner want to sell at the highest possible price.
  - The investor will want you to give as much as possible in the form of **Representations and Warranties** while you will likely want to give little more than the bare minimum.

> Whoever loses their cool generally loses the argument.

There are many other points at which the negotiation might become quite adversarial. The crux of adversarial situations is that whoever loses their cool generally loses the argument. This is one of the reasons people use litigation or divorce lawyers, real estate agents, and so on, to act as buffers in the negotiation process. Your financial and legal advisors will be your most important shock absorbers in the potentially adversarial situation of negotiating the sale of your company.

- *Intermediary:* The use of an independent third party may help overcome the adversarial nature of the sale process and help create a win-win situation for all parties. An independent intermediary is uniquely positioned to understand the thinking of all parties to the **Transaction,** and if that independent intermediary is also a master at structuring Transactions, he or she should have considerable leeway to structure solutions that will be acceptable to all.

Remember, the purpose of external advisors is to make you—the owner—and your entire management team look good by anticipating issues before they arise and by preparing disclosure in a professional manner. Good advisors should bring trust and professionalism to the process. Ultimately, if investors believe that your company has capable management, and that the information you provide can be trusted, this will have a positive effect on the valuation.

Small-business owners are often trapped: if you are trying to sell a company that is worth $1 or $2 million, it will be very challenging to find the quality of expertise that you might like to have at a price that is affordable. Transactions in this order of magnitude are often advised only by a legal advisor, possibly with some assistance from the company's auditor or accountant. For large Transactions (e.g., over $100 million), the investor often comes to the **Due Diligence** with a team of dozens of staff and advisors, including high-powered legal advisors, financial advisors, auditors, and tax advisors.

> Be aware of potential conflicts of interest at advisor level when you are selling your business.

Be aware of potential conflicts of interest at advisor level when you are selling your business. For example, I have seen a few cases where in-house advisors, who have been with the company for years, and who derive a substantial percentage of their revenue from their client, resisted Transactions, presumably because they feared losing one of their most important clients. You may find yourself experiencing overt or covert resistance to a Transaction, above and beyond what protection of your interests might dictate. This resistance usually involves some kind of hidden agenda, where the advisor will not be particularly upset if your Transaction fails!

You might say there are two contradictory principles in selecting your advisory team: on the one hand, you want the best team money will buy, to position you strongly vis-à-vis the investors, but there must also be some proportionality between your advisory budget and the size of your Transaction. The size of the team that you build will depend on the size and complexity of your company and the envisaged Transaction. You should aim to at least achieve negotiating parity with the investors. Remember that if you don't successfully close the Transaction, you may still have to pay substantial advisory fees.

## COMPOSITION AND ROLE OF YOUR TEAM

We'll now get into the roles of the most important advisors in a typical sale or business Transaction, and I'll give you a few tips on how to select them.

### The Legal Advisor

There are many legal dimensions to a Transaction:

1. *Information disclosure to investors:* The process of selling a company or raising capital involves an enormous amount of information transfer

to investors, whether in the **Information Memorandum (IM)**, **Data Room**, or just questions answered informally. At a minimum, a legal advisor should prepare or at least review all information disclosed to investors that is of a legal nature (e.g., information on ownership and clean title to real estate, assets; information about the regulatory environment in which your company operates; and information about any litigation in which your company is involved). You may, as a matter of prudence, also wish to have your legal advisor review all material information passed on to an investor.

2. *Deal structuring:* Should the investor purchase assets or shares? Should the investment be by way of injection of fresh capital into the company? Is an **Earn-Out** appropriate, and if so, how should it be structured? Skilled legal advisors are experts on the legal aspects of structuring Transactions.

3. *Drafting legal agreements:* There are numerous legal agreements that may be required in the course of a Transaction: confidentiality agreements, **Term Sheets**, employment agreements, **Shareholders' Agreements**, noncompete agreements, and the **Sale and Purchase Agreement (SPA)**. Of these, the SPA is typically the most crucial and the most difficult, especially the portion pertaining to Representations and Warranties, limitations to such liabilities, and implications of any breach. In other words, if you, as the owner of a business, sell all or a portion of the shares of a company, you will usually need to represent and warrant that the information provided represents full, true, and plain disclosure, and that there were no errors or omissions in the Data Room, and possibly in the IM or other documents as well. The investor will typically reserve the right to claw back all or a significant portion of the purchase price in the event that there were any material errors or omissions.

4. *Satisfying conditions for closing:* The SPA will typically contain several conditions that must be satisfied. Typically, these are to be met by the seller, but there may also be conditions for the investor to meet. The legal advisors for the seller and the investor typically orchestrate the entire closing procedure, which can involve the simultaneous signatures of dozens or hundreds of documents and transfers of funds.

> A significant portion of your purchase price, and how much of it you can ultimately keep, depends on your legal advisor.

A significant portion of your purchase price, and how much of it you can ultimately keep, depends on your legal advisor. Select your legal advisor carefully: someone you know and feel that you can rely on. Don't hire a mercenary, but someone you can really trust; someone with sound judgment who will give you good advice. But don't let the pendulum swing too far to the other side either: one of the most common mistakes business owners make is to select a legal advisor with whom they have a long-standing relationship who may have little or no transactional experience (e.g., the company's general commercial counsel). This is no more appropriate than asking your general commercial counsel to represent you in a divorce hearing. The legal advisor you select should have acted in at least five to ten Transactions. This is a minimum: dozens would be even better. Try to find out your legal advisor's track record with respect to those Transactions. Did the Transactions close successfully? Get some references. Now is not the time to be shy.

Another important point: your transactional legal advisor should be an excellent negotiator. Often the negotiation on Representations and Warranties is tougher and more challenging than negotiating the price. All the legal knowledge in the world is of limited use unless your legal advisor is capable of projecting that knowledge and achieving positive results in negotiations.

Should you hire a sole practitioner or a law firm? Larger Transactions definitely require an entire legal team, and hence require the services of a law firm. In such cases, you should select one lawyer within the firm and ensure that he or she personally has the requisite credentials and that he or she will personally supervise all work and be present at all important meetings. (I have seen it happen a few times where the law firm hired by my client sent a junior lawyer rather than the senior partner to a crucial SPA negotiation.)

It is important to find a legal advisor who does not feel compelled to participate in or influence the commercial aspects of the deal, aspects which should be left to the principals and their financial advisors, unless you specifically request otherwise. And your legal advisor should not only point out the risks involved in any Transaction, but also be capable of offering solutions in risk management; for example, through creative deal structuring.

> Your choice of legal advisor is one of the most important decisions you will make in determining the success of your Transaction.

In short, your legal advisor can make a tremendous difference between your Transaction closing or not closing; between your becoming embroiled in litigation or staying clear of it; and between a substantial portion of your purchase price being clawed back by the investor or not. Your choice of legal advisor is one of the most important decisions you will make in determining the success of your Transaction.

## The Accountant

While the legal advisor covers the legal dimension of a Transaction, the accountant or auditor handles the accountancy dimension of the exercise. The accountant typically reviews all information given to investors that is of an accounting nature (in the IM and Data Room). There will likely be a number of questions on the accounting information in the Data Room, which the accountant should be on standby to help answer. The SPA is likely to contain a number of annexes that are of an accounting nature, which should also be reviewed by the accountant. For example, if there is a purchase price adjustment clause (i.e., if shareholders' equity, working capital, cash, or other measures deviate from the expected level at closing), or if the parties negotiate an Earn-Out, the accountant is likely to have an extremely important role in defining the parameters to be monitored and their levels during the negotiation of the SPA, and then monitoring those parameters both at and after closing.

Every country has different professional designations for accountants (e.g., Certified Public Accountant (CPA) in the United States, Associated Chartered Accountant (ACA) in the United Kingdom, Chartered Accountant (CA) in Scotland or Canada, or the Association of Chartered Certified Accountants (ACCA), a globally recognized certification). Conduct your research to determine the appropriate designations in your country. At least as important as the professional designations, however, is whether the person heading your accountancy team has experience on at least five or ten Transactions of a similar nature.

## The Taxation Expert

Ultimately, your goal as shareholder should be not to maximize Transaction revenues, but to maximize *after-tax* Transaction revenues. The role of the taxation expert is instrumental in achieving this, and may save you millions.

> Too many business owners begin to think of tax planning just before or after signing the SPA. This is too late.

Too many business owners begin to think of tax planning just before or after signing the SPA. This is too late. You will have much more flexibility in tax planning and maximizing after-tax Transaction revenues if you consult with your tax advisor during the Business Exit Planning process. This is the stage at which the tax advisor can also best make a significant contribution to your estate planning efforts, if you are engaged in estate planning.

In the Business Exit Planning phase, your tax advisor can help in the following areas:

1. Identifying possible skeletons in the closet from a taxation perspective and solving them to the extent possible prior to going to market with the company.
2. Advising on the possible advantages of a holding company structure; helping to determine the best structure and jurisdiction of the entities; and beginning to implement the structure.
3. Analyzing taxation dimensions of estate planning issues.
4. Giving advance advice on the Transaction structure that would best accomplish your objectives from a tax-efficiency point of view.

During the transactional phase, your tax advisor could provide assistance in the following areas:

- Reviewing all information related to taxation that goes into the Data Room.
- Identifying taxation issues and solving them, if possible.
- Answering investors' questions that pertain to taxation during the Data Room.
- Advising on taxation aspects of Transaction structuring during negotiation of the Term Sheet and SPA.

Once again, your taxation expert should have advised on at least five to ten comparable Transactions. Some clients prefer their taxation expert and their accounting expert to be one and the same. You should be aware that in some jurisdictions (e.g., France, Croatia, Italy) this is not permitted, because of potential conflict of interest.

## The Financial Advisor

A financial advisor, like a legal advisor, may be an effective advocate of your interests and provide valuable advice that can make the difference between the success and failure of a Transaction. A financial advisor can also provide advice, the implications of which may be measured in millions of dollars. As the name implies, the financial advisor looks after the financial (as opposed to the accounting) dimension of the exercise, including:

- *Business exit planning and valuation of your company:* Your financial advisor is probably best equipped to advise you on Business Exit Planning, and coordinating a team of advisors in assisting you with your plan. The valuation will usually include building a Business Plan, estimating cash flow for at least the next five years, and conducting a comparables valuation.

- *Preparing information disclosure:* Your financial advisor will probably be the member of your team best equipped to anticipate what the investor's information requirements are likely to be, and then to prepare the necessary information (**Teaser**, IM, Data Room, and **Management Presentation**).

- *Designing and running a process:* Assuming your financial advisor has the necessary experience, he or she should be best prepared to advise you on the various exit options you might consider (**IPO**, sale to strategic or financial investors, **MBO**, etc.), as well as on the type of process you should be running. Should it be a fully competitive process, and if so, what kind? Who should be invited to bid? What kind of prequalification criteria, if any, should be established? How should issues of confidentiality be handled during the process?

- *Acting as a negotiator and intermediary:* Your financial advisor should be an extremely strong negotiator and communicator. While the financial advisor may come up with a proposed valuation for your company, what the investor ultimately accepts may be greater than or less than the hypothetical value put forward in a valuation. This depends, to a great degree, on the financial advisor's strength as a negotiator. A financial advisor should fully understand the motivations and interests of all parties, so as to structure win-win solutions. As an effective intermediary, he or she should be able to bring the parties into line if necessary, resolve blockages during the negotiations, and catalyze the final closing.

**Special Considerations in Hiring a Financial Advisor**   There seems to be a pattern of questions that that reveals a lack of understanding of the limitations of the role of a financial advisor. I can suggest three principles that you might apply when hiring your financial advisor:

1. **Don't expect a financial advisor to estimate the value of your company before he or she is hired:** The potential for error in such a rapid, back-of-the-envelope valuation is enormous. A thorough valuation usually

requires the use of multiple methods. A quick valuation is done solely on the basis of multiples, making it typically much less reliable than **Discounted Cash Flow** (DCF). Furthermore, when you apply multiples to perform a valuation, there is a risk of magnifying the error if you are multiplying the wrong number. For example, if your business is valued at six times cash flow and you, as the owner, pay yourself a salary that is $100,000 below market salary, your company will be overvalued by approximately $600,000. The financial statements of a company must be carefully examined before applying multiples. Furthermore, there may be a number of factors unknown to an advisor who has not had the chance to look at a company thoroughly. What if there is litigation or a threat of litigation against the company? What if the company is about to lose its most important client? What if there is new technology on the horizon that is about to disrupt the industry? In any one of these cases, a quick valuation is likely to be grossly inaccurate.

So how should you handle the issue of valuation when hiring an advisor? Ask questions that ensure that your potential advisor thoroughly understands the principles of valuation and has experience in the subject. If your decision to proceed with a Transaction depends on the valuation, valuation could be the first priority of your financial advisor once he or she is on board. Your decision to proceed with the Transaction could be conditional on the advisor arriving at a threshold valuation.

> If the company starts down the road of negotiating with one investor, it becomes more and more difficult to bring other potential investors into the process.

2. **Don't ask an advisor to introduce an investor before you give him or her a mandate:** Occasionally, a client will ask an advisor to bring a potential investor to the table before giving the advisor a mandate. This is usually a mistake, for two reasons. First, in the event of the investor being interested, the company will typically be completely unprepared to follow through (i.e., it will be unable to provide the interested investor with the huge amount of information he or she is likely to require, which typically requires months of preparation). Second, if the company starts down the road of negotiating with one investor, it becomes more and more difficult to bring other potential investors into the process. In this way, the company foregoes the possibility of entering into a truly competitive process, a process that usually has the effect of driving up

price, improving the terms and conditions of a Transaction, and increasing the likelihood of closing it.

So what should you do? If your trusted advisor believes that your company is saleable with the proper preparation, allow him or her to help prepare your company appropriately, and then bring investors to the table in a competitive process.

3. **It is better if you hire your financial advisor at the beginning of Business Exit Planning, rather than just prior to a Transaction:** Going through a Business Exit Planning process prior to putting your company on the market has number of important benefits:

- You will have a better idea of your exit options (sale of a minority or majority of shares, MBO, IPO, etc.) and the valuations that might be achieved under each scenario.

- You will have had an opportunity to better understand your company's value drivers, how investors are likely to perceive its strengths and weaknesses, and the marketing strategy you need to take your company to market.

- You will have a better idea of what value enhancements may be possible prior to taking your company to market, as well as identifying possible skeletons in the closet.

**Contractual Aspects of Engaging Your Financial Advisor**  Here are three things to look out for when engaging your financial advisor:

1. **Expect your advisor to ask for exclusivity:** It is very damaging to the reputation of your firm, as well as that of your advisor, if multiple advisors are calling upon the same potential investor. This is virtually impossible to explain to the investor. It makes your marketing effort seem chaotic and very unprofessional. It is also likely to lead to disputes and possible litigation with respect to payment of success fees.

> If you pay peanuts, you'll get monkeys.

2. **Don't expect an advisor to work for a success fee only:** As the saying goes: if you pay peanuts, you'll get monkeys. As in any hiring situation, ensure that the individual or company you are hiring is appropriately motivated. Given that you, as owner, will usually have the liberty, at any point in a Transaction, of refusing any offer, or indeed even calling off a Transaction, an advisor working on a success fee alone is unlikely

to invest the time necessary to do a thorough job or may be motivated only to skim the cream (e.g., try to opportunistically close a Transaction with just the bare minimum of preparation or proactive marketing). This will seldom be in your best interest.

3. **Your advisor's fee should be a retainer plus a success fee calculated as a percentage of the Transaction proceeds:** Your fees will likely be a combination of fixed fees (retainer) and variable fees (success fee). The Business Exit Planning exercise is probably best structured as a fixed fee; the mandate to carry out a Transaction is probably best compensated by a fixed-fee component accompanied by a success fee. The fixed fee will motivate the advisor to give full attention, care, and effort to deliverables such as the IM, the Business Plan and valuation, and the Data Room. The success fee, which should be calculated as a percentage of the Transaction proceeds, should motivate your advisor to perform a truly proactive and competitive marketing effort, as well as negotiate in your best interests to maximize the Transaction proceeds.

## SELECTING ADVISORS: AN OVERVIEW

Table 4.1 summarizes the roles of various advisors in the Business Exit Planning and transactional phases.

Please note that advisors do not work independently in any of these activities, but work in close consultation with you, and under your direction.

You may want to hire and supervise each advisor independently, or you may want to appoint one of them as the lead advisor, to lead or at least coordinate the entire advisory team. The latter option has a couple of advantages:

1. It will save you the time you would have spent managing each advisor individually.
2. There are a number of issues that may fall between the cracks among several advisors; conversely, a number of issues may transcend the competencies of multiple advisors. Once again, it takes time to manage these, and generally, these sorts of issues are better managed by someone who has already performed numerous Transactions.

Most of the time, the advisor who is best equipped to play the role of lead advisor would be either your legal advisor or your financial advisor. Which of the two do you trust more? Who has the better leadership and people management capabilities? Who has the necessary time available? The cost element should also be considered.

**TABLE 4.1** Overview of the roles of advisors during the Business Exit Planning and transactional processes

| | Accountant | Legal Advisor | Tax Advisor | Corporate Finance Advisor | Other Advisors |
|---|---|---|---|---|---|
| Business Exit Planning | | | | | |
| Establish objectives of the owner, the company, and the owner's family with respect to business exit | | | | X | |
| Business Plan and valuation | | | | X | |
| Conduct estate planning | | | | | Estate Planner |
| Enhance business performance | | | | X | |
| Develop strategy for avoiding taxes | (x) | (x) | X | (x) | |
| Examine need for insurance | | | | | Insurance Expert |
| Develop strategy for investing proceeds | | | | | Asset Management Expert or Financial Planner |
| Develop Business Exit strategy | (x) | (x) | (x) | X | |
| Prepare teaser, IM, and Data Room | (x) | (x) | | X | |
| Manage sale process | | x | | X | |
| Negotiate Term Sheet | (x) | (x) | (x) | X | |
| Negotiate SPA | (x) | X | (x) | (x) | |
| Close Transaction | (x) | X | | (x) | |

X  Plays the leading role
x  Plays a role
(x)  Plays a supporting role only

## YOUR ADVISORS' ETHICAL STANDARDS

Over the past decade of operating Euro-Phoenix, I have encountered relatively few instances where a financial advisory firm knowingly breached laws, or industry or ethical standards; instances of overt contravention are relatively few and far between. This does not mean that users of corporate finance advisory services should just assume that the issue of ethics is not important. Ethics are of paramount importance and ethical issues may arise on a number of occasions:

**Potential conflicts of interest on Due Diligence of a buy-side mandate:**
Several years ago, I was working on the buy side of a cable TV mandate. I uncovered some hidden liabilities in the target company. I did not hesitate for a second to disclose this to our client, knowing full well that he would withdraw from pursuing the target company, and that we were eliminating the possibility of a success fee. If you think about it, you will realize that any advisor on the buy side of a mandate that is remunerated by a success fee has a similar potential conflict.

**Setting fees:** Fee structures agreed to with advisors should be fully aligned with your interests as the client. For example, if you hire an advisor to buy a company for you and offer him or her a success fee based on a percentage of the purchase price, your advisor may have a conflict of interest. The higher the purchase price negotiated, the higher the success fee will be...think about it! In my experience, a predefined lump sum fee works best in such circumstances. Success fees defined as a percentage of Transaction value work well where an advisor is helping you sell a company or raise capital—in such instances the higher the valuation achieved, the higher the success fee will be.

**Collecting a fee on the other side of a Transaction:** Euro-Phoenix was once engaged in selling a major asset for a multinational corporation. Four offers were received. Three of those offers came with explicit bribes from the offering investors. If we helped ensure that a particular investor obtained the asset and worked on driving the price down rather than up, then the investor would be willing to pay us a success fee even larger than that offered by our client. When this concern was expressed to one particular investor, he hastened to add: "Don't worry. You can collect the success fee rom your client as well!" Are you sure that your advisor will resist temptation? Some jurisdictions (e.g., the United Kingdom) specifically forbid financial advisors collecting fees on both sides of a Transaction.

**Where a financial advisor is also in the private equity business:** Can you be sure that there are strong Chinese walls* in place (e.g., that information will not pass between the advisory and private equity sides of the business)? I am aware of one situation where a private equity firm which was related to a particular financial advisory firm made an acquisition in the cable TV area. Whereas previously the advisory firm had had a vibrant business in the cable TV sector, to the best of my knowledge it never achieved another mandate in that sector, because the owners or managers of cable TV firms could not be fully confident that their confidential information would not end up in the hands of a competitor.

**When a financial advisor also provides audit or other services to a client:** In a number of jurisdictions, it is forbidden by law for a firm that provides audit services to a client to provide financial advisory services or any other services to the same client. (The United States, the United Kingdom, and France, for example, have restrictive regimes, preventing audit firms from deriving non-audit fees from audit clients.) The potential conflicts of interest are numerous. Obtaining a generous success fee on a corporate finance mandate could provide just the right incentive to be more flexible with respect to some sticky points in the audit.

> Your advisors' ethics are at least as important as their knowledge and technical skills.

Some food for thought, isn't it? While I might focus mostly on my own industry—the financial advisory industry—similar ethical issues are prevalent for legal, accounting, taxation, and other advisors. Your advisors' ethics are at least as important as their knowledge and technical skills. If you don't already know the advisors with whom you plan to work, check their references.

---

* In business, a Chinese wall or firewall is an information barrier implemented within a firm to separate and isolate persons who make investment decisions from persons who are privy to undisclosed material information which may influence those decisions. This is a way of avoiding conflict of interest problems.

# CHAPTER 5

# Building a Business with Sustainable Value

*Don't congratulate us when we buy a company. Any fool can buy a company. Congratulate us when we sell it and we've done something with it and created real value.*

—Henry Kravis (b. 1944)
American financier and investor

One of the most common reasons **Transactions** fail is that owners believe they have created more value (often measured by their own time, effort, or money invested), which is not perceived the same way by investors. But even for owners who have a valuable business, as mentioned in the Introduction, a common error is to put their company on the market without adequate preparation.

In this chapter, I will deal in considerably more detail with the need to build sustainable value, and to prepare your business prior to a Transaction, covering the following subjects:

- the importance of looking at your business from an investor's perspective
- clarifying and adjusting corporate strategy
- corporate governance, systems, and the "one-man show"
- pre-Transaction restructuring
- identify and manage risks
- operational improvements to enhance the value of a business
- the need to properly structure and document non-arm's-length transactions

Let's look at each of the above subjects individually.

## LOOK AT YOUR BUSINESS FROM AN INVESTOR'S PERSPECTIVE

The value of your business is ultimately what an investor will pay for it in an arm's length Transaction.* Some owner/managers of businesses lack objectivity in assessing their own businesses, the way parents sometimes lack objectivity in assessing their own children. The value of a business often bears little relation to the amount of money or effort invested in it, which all too often governs the owner's perspective (see Box 5.1).

It's good to bring in a fresh pair of eyes, someone who can look at your business objectively. Few people are better qualified to do this than seasoned investment bankers or corporate finance advisors, people experienced in these areas who have dealt with hundreds of investors, and who know and can anticipate the views the investors will take on the company in question. A valuation is not the application of a standard formula; it requires experienced and considered judgement.

---

### BOX 5.1    GAS DISTRIBUTION BUSINESS

The government of an Asian country had invested more than $3 billion in building its gas distribution infrastructure. The company worked relatively efficiently, had modern equipment, and was considered the crown jewel in the government's privatization program.

The government was in for a bit of a shock when its investment bankers told it their estimated value of the business: negative $400 million! "How could this possibly be?" fumed the Privatization Minister.

The company was selling at a regulated price, at which it lost money on every cubic meter of natural gas sold. Under such circumstances, there was no way an investor would give a positive valuation of the company! Sellers, and not just governments, often have an inflated value of their holdings. What you have invested in your company in terms of time and money has little correlation to what an investor may be willing to pay for it.

---

* An arm's length transaction is one that is between parties that are completely non-related and independent. Where such is not the case, a transaction may be considered non-arm's length. A non-arm's-length transaction may be on commercial or non-commercial terms.

A valuation is not the application of a standard formula; it requires experienced and considered judgement.

A good place to start for a fresh perspective on your business might be a SWOT analysis—an analysis of its Strengths, Weaknesses, Opportunities, and Threats—viewed by an independent party. Doing a SWOT analysis is like looking in a mirror. You might not like what you see, but if your financial advisor sees your business in a certain light, chances are that investors will not see your company in a better light. If the SWOT analysis concludes that your company has certain weaknesses (e.g., inventory turns and your receivables collection are slow by industry standards), you'll have the opportunity to work on those perceived weaknesses before putting your company on the market. If you put your company on the market having cured these weaknesses, it will be worth more.

## CLARIFYING AND ADJUSTING CORPORATE STRATEGY

Most owners of mid-sized businesses seem to have an implicit strategy, but seldom in writing. If you ask them, they will often say "it's in my head". This may be a big mark against the business in the eyes of an investor, as it is evidence that the owner is running the company in an ad hoc fashion, rather than a management team running it systematically.

Different strategists will have different approaches to putting together a strategy, but a strategic plan will typically contain the following elements or address the following issues:

- Corporate vision, mission, and objectives, backed up by a three to five year business plan (see Chapter 6), with assumptions documented.
- What distinguishes the company from its competitors? What is the company's unique selling proposition?
- How sustainable is this uniqueness or positioning over time? What are barriers to entry? Does the company own intellectual property or brands which help sustain the company's advantage?
- What are the risks inherent in the business? These risks would include the risks of new competitors, disruptive behavior by competitors, risk from new technologies, and so on. Does management understand these risks and have a strategy for managing these risks?

- What are the "value drivers" of the company? (e.g., how does the company create value?) This is fundamental to the company's business model; I will return to this subject shortly.
- What does the company do to create a healthy corporate culture and a learning environment? What are core competencies, and are these competencies "cutting edge" today, and likely to remain such tomorrow?

The advantages of putting your corporate strategy in writing include the need to communicate the strategy widely within the firm, so as to create alignment, as well as to sharpen thinking and create debate, helping to further evolve the strategy. In fast-moving industries, strategy may evolve extremely rapidly, where an entirely new strategy or business model may be required every few years.

Most investors will ask you for a written summary of your strategy. A written strategy is an indication that there is not just an implicit framework in the owner or CEO's head, but a coherent strategy that represents a consensus within the management team that has been communicated broadly. Conversely, the lack of a written strategy may indicate that the firm has no strategy, or that it is "half-baked." If the company does not have a good strategy, there is a high probability that cash flows cannot be sustained or grown, and possibly also that the company is a "one man show." Putting a strategy in writing, and debating the subject among the management team, tends to sharpen minds. A written strategy should be an evolving document, evolving as management thinking advances on the subject.

An adjustment to the strategic focus of the firm can sometimes make an enormous difference to the value generation potential of the firm (see Box 5.2).

> Every firm has a business model, ways in which it generates value. In corporate finance jargon, these are known as value drivers.

Every firm has a business model, ways in which it generates value. In corporate finance jargon, these are known as value drivers. A financial advisor can help you understand exactly what value drivers drive the value of your business. Once you have a better understanding of these value drivers, you will be in a much better position to build your business (as per the example of the media company below).

---

## BOX 5.2   A MEDIA FIRM

A particular media firm focused on two markets: weekly glossy magazines and web portals. Most of its efforts were directed at developing the glossy magazines. It had a number of portals that were quite good (for selling used cars, etc.) in addition to a first mover advantage and a strong brand, but it had neglected the portal business in favor of the glossy weekly magazine.

We informed the client of the dynamics of the magazine *vs.* portal markets in its geographic region: every dollar of revenue generated in the portal market would generate *seven times* the value of what one dollar of revenue in the magazine publication business would produce.

It became very apparent that this was where the company needed to focus for the next few years, yet it was very reluctant to do so, to the point where the company broke off discussions with us about selling the company in the near term. No matter. I have every confidence that when the time comes, our client will come back to us, and it will be a win-win for all concerned.

---

Another example: in the direct marketing business, if you establish that it costs you $100 to contact 100 prospects, and 2 percent of them respond to your proposition, bringing a total of $500 revenue and $260 cash flow to your business, it makes sense to roll out the model until your returns diminish.

## CORPORATE GOVERNANCE, SYSTEMS, AND THE ONE-MAN SHOW

Many small and mid-sized companies are run by dominant owner-managers. Most of these individuals are dynamic, creative, driven entrepreneurs; many have built significant enterprises from the ground up. With boundless energy and a detailed understanding of their businesses, they often substitute an entire level of management as well as the need for complex and costly systems, meaning that their businesses are often very profitable. I refer to such owner-managers as one-man shows: a phenomenon that is very common in medium-sized, owner-managed businesses. (Of course, it could equally be a one-woman show!)

> Businesses run by one-man shows often run into challenges when trying to grow or engage in any type of exit

Yet businesses run by one-man shows often run into challenges when trying to grow or engage in any type of exit. This has to do with the real or perceived risks of conducting Transactions with such companies:

- Should a one-man show become sick or incapacitated or leave the firm, the firm may become ungovernable or lose profitability. In this event, key relationships with clients, staff, or suppliers may be lost, causing further disruption, which may substantially add to the risk associated with investing in a particular enterprise.
- Executing a Transaction, in particular satisfying the informational requirements of a **Due Diligence** and managing a complex negotiation, often requires the collective efforts of a team. A one-man show may become a bottleneck, simply incapable of handling the daily operations on top of the demands placed on him by the Transaction.
- Businesses run by one-man shows frequently lack the systems (whether IT platforms, accounting systems, or corporate governance procedures) that can sustain profitable growth beyond a certain point. The methodology behind the company's operations may exist only inside the head of the one-man show, or have been jotted down on the back of an envelope, or have been left in a spreadsheet, never having been communicated throughout the organization. The lack of such systems makes the potential loss of one key individual all the more difficult for the enterprise to bear. More importantly, it also creates various limitations to growth. This will most definitely impact valuation. Business owners should be particularly careful of projecting past rates of growth into the future without making appropriate investments in systems and staffing.
- Businesses run by one-man shows often lack the internal communications (daily, weekly, quarterly meetings) required to exchange the necessary information, so that all team members can function efficiently. If the one-man show is absent, the efficiency can drop further—and dramatically.

Of course, whether a business is run by a one-man show is seldom a clear-cut question. When assessing an acquisition target, an investor will assess the degree to which the target is run by a one-man show, as it may have a serious impact on the valuation (e.g., in a **Discounted Cash Flow (DCF)** model, the appropriate investments to sustain growth should be reflected). I have seen numerous instances where this has been a deal-breaker. In fact, this is one of the most frequent deal-breakers with small and mid-sized companies (even though the investor may be more diplomatic when giving reasons for breaking off negotiations). One of the reasons that larger firms are typically more attractive to investors than smaller firms is that they are less beholden to one owner/manager, and have better systems, processes, and management systems in place. Similarly, publicly traded, stock-exchange-listed firms typically trade at higher multiples than owner-managed firms, in part because they have greater depth and breadth of management.

> Is it yourself you are trying to sell, or your business?

What can a one-man show do to avoid diminishing the valuation of his firm, or even himself becoming a deal-breaker? In a nutshell, he can empower people within the organization and build systems. This is easier said than done and may run counter to the personality of the owner/manager, who often enjoys exerting a high degree of control. Some owner/managers are so dominant that they are unable to attract into their immediate circle of direct reports individuals who are themselves highly empowered and capable of making decisions independently. However, perhaps the realization that empowering people and building systems may add substantially to his own net worth may provide the one-man show with sufficient financial incentive to consider such a course of action. Bottom line: is it yourself you are trying to sell, or your business?

So if your goal is not to sell yourself, but a company, what kind of corporate governance improvements should you consider? Corporate governance is about creating an alignment of the interests of all stakeholders, based on targets, information, transparency, and accountability. Strategy and objectives should be formulated and communicated throughout the organization, with clear measurements that allow for complete accountability.

There is no magic formula for what constitutes good corporate governance. This will depend on the size of the company, the sector, the nature of activities, and to some degree, the personalities of the parties. Some of the elements that might be considered important (often inter-related with each other) include:

- *Board of Directors:* A good Board will provide you with considerable advice on a wide variety of subjects. It is particularly helpful if there are at least a few independent members of the Board; independent in terms of not depending financially on the company, as well as being willing to express their ideas independently. The Board may also have certain committees, which will handle issues such as compensation of senior management, succession, audit, and so on. A properly constituted Board might also provide a solution for leading the firm, should an owner/manager become incapacitated for whatever reason. Where the legal form of the company does not permit a Board of Directors, you might consider an Advisory Committee.
- *Definition of structures and roles:* A good organizational chart, with clearly defined roles, responsibilities, and job descriptions, is conducive to building value. These are considered basic to good governance and achieving sustainable growth.
- *Internal controls:* Does the company have a set of internal controls, where specific individuals are monitoring other individuals with accountability, to ensure observance of laws, reliability of financial reporting, observance of internal procedures, and so on? Internal controls are necessary to ensure that assets are not stolen, and that the assets are being used efficiently and effectively.
- *Quality control:* An ISO (International Organization for Standardization) quality control system is usually a must, particularly for companies that produce physical goods. What is the scope of the ISO that you might wish to implement? I once encountered a company that boasted of having an ISO; it turned out that the ISO was applicable only to the operation of its receivables system. There are also industry-specific quality standards. Companies in the food business, for example, generally adopt the HACCP (Hazards Analysis and Critical Control Points) designation. General Electric was famous for its implementation of Six Sigma. Choose standards that are appropriate for your industry and company, that bring value to your clients or are required by law.
- *Internal policies and procedures:* To what extent are the policies and procedures of the company documented? Is it all in your head as the owner/manager, or do staff members have the ability to read and refer to them at their leisure? Does the company have a comprehensive Staff Manual? Is there an induction system for training new staff with respect to the company's policies and procedures?
- *Dashboard:* Is there also a dashboard to monitor performance of various parts of the company? The company should carefully determine its key performance indicators, which are essential to building value, and monitor these over time. Management, along with the Board,

## BOX 5.3   A CONSTRUCTION COMPANY

Euro-Phoenix had progressed well with the sale of a particular construction company. Several investors had expressed serious interest and were proceeding with Due Diligence. There was one purchaser in particular who was more motivated and willing to pay a significantly higher price than the others. But this investor insisted on seeing a margin calculation for every single project that the company had taken on over the past three years as a condition for proceeding. The company did not have the IT systems in place to automatically calculate these numbers. Hence we had to stop the Transaction for approximately 10 weeks, while a team of three people manually calculated the margins on each project. This caused additional complications because during those 10 weeks, the company won certain new contracts and lost an existing contract, which created a very tough contract renegotiation. It is better to have the necessary information going into Due Diligence, rather than having to generate information or data during the process.

should be aware if performance of one part of the company is flagging, preferably sooner rather than later. The dashboard should tie into performance reviews and bonuses for staff.

- *Management accounting:* The company should not only produce financial statements for tax purposes, but also statements and analysis that provide the management and Board with all the information they need to know about the economic performance of their company. This might include:

  - Appropriate profit centers or cost centers provided by the accounting system, so that the company is aware of how it is performing in its different lines of business, or even each contract (see Box 5.3).
  - A budgeting/pricing system that accurately prices new contracts.
  - A system that actually monitors the profitability of each contract, product, and client. How much money did the company make or lose on each contract, product or client? How did that compare with the budgeting/pricing? Was the budgeting/pricing accurate?

- *Analysis of capital expenditure:* A DCF analysis may be performed on each major capital expenditure. This will provide management with information on the economic rationality of various capital expenditures, and permit a certain amount of prioritization.

- *Code of ethics:* Does the company have a code of ethics? If so, to what degree is it adopted and internalized by staff?
- *IT and other systems:* Businesses evolve as they grow. When someone starts a business and is the sole employee, by necessity the company must be a one-man show. As the business grows to dozens, then hundreds, of employees, however, the company's systems must evolve to keep pace with growth and lay the foundation for future growth. The creation and implementation of these systems often cause severe growing pains. The lack of these systems may cause quality problems, create irate customers, or cause so much stress for staff members that they leave. Depending on the nature of the company's activities, you may wish to implement a number of Enterprise Resource Planning (ERP) modules:
  - The Customer Relationship Management (CRM) module is particularly valuable for sales-oriented companies or companies that give priority to high-quality customer care.
  - The Supply Chain Management (SCM) module includes a range of software tools used in executing supply chain transactions, managing supplier relationships and controlling associated business processes.
  - The Access Control module provides for the management of user privileges for various processes.

Also, an investor will often look at the robustness of the company's systems for backup and disaster recovery. Of course, these steps should be taken in light of a cost/benefit analysis.

Letting go or delegating can be tremendously difficult for entrepreneurs. Yet it is the prerequisite for growth, as without delegation you will become a bottleneck in your company. In my opinion, delegation should never be blind. It requires three elements:

> Delegation should never be blind.

1. A clear definition of the delegation (whether a job description, terms of reference, etc.), along with the objectives (preferably in quantifiable and measurable terms), resources available, systems which might assist the task, and timeline.
2. An identification of the right individual(s) who are capable of fulfilling the delegated tasks and responsibilities.

3. Monitoring the results, a feedback loop. If results are achieved consistently, the feedback loop or monitoring might be loosened.

Delegation is a skill. If you are missing any one of these three elements, you might believe you are delegating when, in fact, you are abdicating responsibility. Or, even if you have all three elements in place, you may still continue to micro-manage, thereby interfering with the delegation.

You might ask why your company should go to the extensive effort required to introduce good corporate governance (see Box 5.4).

*Effective Corporate Governance improves investor confidence that the assets they have provided to a company are used for the intended purpose. Therefore, employing best practices in Corporate Governance should increase access to capital...This association is based on good governance's ability to lower risk, inherent in a project or company, and in parallel increase its attractiveness, or similarly, to lower the expected rate of return investors/lenders demand for investing/lending. Better governance is therefore thought to increase the value of companies. A recent joint McKinsey and World Bank (Global Corporate Governance Forum) study suggests that investors will pay up to a 30 percent premium for companies with good governance...*[1]

All the rules or procedures in the world cannot protect you from deliberate malfeasance. There is also an important function for the tone at the top: the example set by the leaders of the company. You!

---

### BOX 5.4   INTRODUCING THE ENGAGEMENT COMMITTEE

In my own company, one of our independent Advisory Committee members came up with the excellent idea of instituting an Engagement Committee. At Engagement Committee meetings, we review every new advisory mandate that we take on, check out potential conflicts and reputational risks of taking on certain clients, and ensure that there is a consistent cost/benefit analysis applicable to all mandates taken on throughout the firm. The Engagement Committee has proven an extremely useful complement to our corporate governance activities.

## PRE-TRANSACTION RESTRUCTURING

Restructuring takes many forms. And once again, as many books could and probably have been written on the subject, I'm just going to categorize and illustrate some of the types of restructuring that you might consider prior to a Transaction.

### Restructuring to Improve Corporate Governance

Picture a situation where a dozen or more companies in a similar industry are owned directly by one individual, as a result of organic growth of the group into different countries. In this type of situation, prior to any Transaction, it will typically make sense to create a holding company that would own the operating companies. Such a company may create a team with all the necessary management functions (marketing, sales, finance, legal, etc.) that may provide governance at the group level. Investors will typically insist on such a holding structure as a precondition for any investment in the group, as they will probably only wish to delegate board member(s) to one entity, rather than a board member to every single entity in the group. Also, a Transaction to purchase one holding company is much simpler than purchasing a myriad of companies from a legal point of view. As owner, you will also likely find other advantages of this type of holding structure, from better risk management to treasury management. Be careful—when rolling individual companies under a holding company, consult a tax advisor to see whether tax liabilities may be triggered.

### Cost Restructuring

It is surprising how many companies do not manage their costs as tightly as they could. Cost restructuring may help improve cash flow and profitability, or indeed, turn the company from a loss-making entity to a profitable concern. This will considerably affect the attractiveness of the business (see Box 5.5).

But investors will look carefully to make sure that the cost reductions are sustainable, that is, that they cut into the fat rather than the muscle of your business. For example, cutting marketing costs may impair the long-term growth of your company. It is generally better to conduct cost restructuring well before taking your company to market. This both diminishes the need to explain everything to potential investors and shows them a track record of sustainability.

## BOX 5.5   ENGINEERING COMPANY RESTRUCTURES COSTS

An engineering company was suffering significant losses. This was due primarily to excess labor costs in relation to the volume of work the company was habitually carrying out. The company was not only able to shed about 25 percent of staff, but also reduced costs related to office space, telephone, and other expenditure, which restored the company to profitability.

All of a sudden, the company became such an attractive proposition that management itself decided to buy it from its multinational owners.

It is generally better to conduct cost restructuring well before taking your company to market.

### Restructuring Real Estate Holdings

More often than not, investors purchasing companies in the production or service sector will not want to purchase extensive real estate holdings. This will be especially true if the real estate held by your company is not related to its core business. Under such circumstances, you should work closely with a tax expert to hive off the real estate into a separate entity. There may be capital gains taxes associated with the real estate transfers, as well as land transfer taxes or other charges (see Box 5.6).

### Restructuring Fragmented Companies

This is a particularly difficult and time-consuming form of restructuring. If your company has too many business lines and does not have critical mass in any or most of those business lines, you may want to consider focusing production on fewer lines where it is likely to achieve a critical mass. What constitutes critical mass is really in the eye of the beholder/investor. Whatever line of business you are operating in, you can usually obtain a pretty good idea of what constitutes critical mass by talking to experts in your industry (see Box 5.7).

## BOX 5.6   COOLING AND REFRIGERATION COMPANY

A company specializing in cooling and refrigeration of industrial premises owned a number of extremely valuable residential building lots in a central location, with panoramic views. These had nothing to do with the core business.

The company had two choices: first, it could de-merge the company into two legal entities, with the cooling and refrigeration business ending up as one legal entity, and the real estate as another. This option would incur reduced land transfer taxes, which were considerable in the jurisdiction in question. The owner opted for the second option, for the company to sell the real estate prior to closing, primarily from an estate planning perspective, because he wanted to transfer the building lots directly to his daughters.

## BOX 5.7   FOOD COMPANY

An investor approached a company making a wide variety of ketchups, mustards, mayonnaise, and approximately a dozen other foodstuffs. Despite the target company being extremely interesting from the point of view of having ketchup and mustard in the desired geographic area, neither the ketchup nor the mustard business was of the desired critical mass, and the dozen other food products were not nearly as desirable (and also lacking critical mass). The investor withdrew from further negotiations, despite the target company being an excellent strategic fit if it were not for the critical mass issue.

### Restructuring Companies That Have Incompatible Business Lines

A company may operate different businesses with one corporate entity, but these businesses may not be particularly compatible with one another. For example, I once had dealings with a company that made corrugated packaging products as well as toilet paper. While you might say that they both qualify as paper products, the chances of selling the two businesses together would indeed be slim. Similarly, I am aware of an ongoing privatization where a government is trying to sell a company that makes PVC products and fertilizer products. Trying to sell this company with both business lines would severely curtail the number of eligible bidders. It would be far better to sell the two companies separately. Of course, there are usually costs associated with de-merging such companies, sometimes quite considerable costs (e.g., where the different businesses share real estate or infrastructure). Alternatively, you could sell at a severe discount to an opportunistic investor who may undertake the legal and operational separation of the businesses, and realize a nice profit in the process.

## Financial Restructuring

Companies that have excessive levels of debt may consider a debt to equity swap, particularly where the debt may be held as a shareholders' loan. Where there are a number of different loans or credit facilities, it may make sense to consider consolidating these into one credit or loan facility prior to going to market. This may also have the advantage of reducing interest charges, as well as lengthening the term of the debt.

> There is little point in restructuring for the sake of restructuring

Whatever type of restructuring is undertaken should be driven from an investor's perspective. Ultimately, if your company is acceptable to an investor in its current form, with no discount in valuation, then there is little point in restructuring for the sake of restructuring. The advice of an independent advisor, who can anticipate the needs of investors, will be invaluable; this may warn you of any possible deal-breakers or discount factors, and if necessary, you can carry out any restructuring necessary prior to going to market. Bear in mind that most restructuring will take many months. It is difficult to have an investor on standby during that length of time. It's better to get it out of the way before entering into discussions with investors, if possible, even to the point of being able to show financial results over a meaningful period of time to investors.

## Superficial Restructuring (Facelift)

Just as you might give your house a fresh coat of paint before putting it on the market, you might consider certain aesthetic improvements to your business, to give it more visual appeal. I advised one company recently to get rid of a substantial amount of scrap just lying around the yard before showing to an investor. As usual, there is a cost/benefit analysis involved. Those companies that have neglected maintenance on their premises for many years are probably the ones who can least afford expenditure in this regard.

## IDENTIFY AND MANAGE RISKS

> Getting out of bed in the morning has its risks, but so does staying in bed.

Getting out of bed in the morning has its risks, but so does staying in bed—you can have a heart attack anytime! The same is true for companies. There is no such thing as a risk-free company. Most investors understand that. With respect to risk, investors, in my experience, are generally looking for three things:

1. To identify and understand the risks involved.
2. To verify whether management has a good understanding of the risks and an effective strategy for dealing with them.
3. To satisfy themselves as to whether the risks may be effectively handled, either with the management strategy or with a strategy developed by the investors.

So as an owner considering the sale of your company, the worst thing you can do is be like an ostrich and stick your head in the sand, trying to pretend that there are no risks. You need to fully understand the risks and develop strategies for dealing with and mitigating them. And you need to be prepared to communicate with investors about those risks. Boxes 5.8 and 5.9 provide some very interesting case studies in risk management (or lack thereof).

As the owner, you may well have been living with these risks for quite some time, and are probably feeling quite comfortable with most of them. The investor, on the other hand, is just getting to know your business. He or she will have a tendency to look at worst-case scenarios, and will take some time to develop that same comfort level. Advisors retained by the investor are paid to identify risks, and their internal risk management procedures generally require that they map out worst-case scenarios.

## BOX 5.8    MEDICAL EQUIPMENT COMPANY

A profitable and growing medical equipment company made components for medical diagnostic equipment. The CEO thought that the company's popularity with a major global concern was a great opportunity, and concentrated on this client to the extent that over 90 percent of revenue came from this one client. This kind of vulnerability to losing a key client deters the vast majority of investors, and contributed to making the company virtually unsaleable.

To date, the owner remains blithely unconcerned about exit. The last I heard, the global company insisted that he sign a right of first refusal as a condition of doing business with them, and he, apparently, didn't see anything wrong with agreeing to this. I was unable to convince him that once he signed the first right of refusal, he would be giving away a substantial percentage of his company's equity value. As the saying goes, you can lead a horse to water, but you cannot make him drink.

## BOX 5.9    ANOTHER CONSTRUCTION COMPANY

Our client withheld one crucial piece of information from us until we were halfway through preparing the **Information Memorandum (IM)**: the company had only one employee (the General Manager), plus several hundred staff members who were working as independent contractors.

The tax laws of the country in question had a much more generous regime for independent contractors than for employees; yet the tax authorities could also reclassify revenues received by independent contractors as employment income, in the event that the independent contractors were not truly independent, but de facto acted as employees. In such a case, the company would have had to pay millions in payroll and social security taxes, not to mention penalties and interest.

Because of this non-disclosure by our client and the non-saleability of the business, we had to withdraw.

The last example is an illustration of what is known as a "skeleton in the closet". This expression usually refers to a risk that is unidentified, or whose significance is not fully understood by the owner, until an investor identifies it and makes an issue out of it. This can be a "worst nightmare" scenario during any Transaction process, as it may completely derail a Transaction.

Do your best to identify these skeletons. Your advisors, who have the benefit of "fresh eyeballs", independence, and experience with investors, may be invaluable. Your success as a business owner/manager depends on your receiving candid, objective feedback from your advisors. Don't shoot the messenger! It is sometimes difficult for advisors to give candid feedback to their clients, who occasionally come across as quite belligerent or hostile when receiving negative feedback. You should do everything possible to encourage an open dialogue. A few clients deliberately withhold information from investors and even their own financial advisors (Box 5.10), often with devastating consequences. This is like withholding information from your legal advisor before going into litigation: it's at your own peril.

Your advisors are there to help you. Every business has its warts and blemishes. Your advisor can help you solve the problem (e.g. if there is a defect on the title of real estate, that defect may often be cured). Or your

---

**BOX 5.10    A U.S. ROBOTICS COMPANY**

A U.S. robotics company was looking to raise a major capital infusion in order to fund technology development and international expansion. The company had retained financial advisors and legal advisors, and had progressed to the point where investors had been identified and were commencing Due Diligence.

At that point, one of the investors became aware that a major piece of litigation had been launched against the company. The owner had not divulged this to either his advisors or to his investors. His explanation was that the litigation was a sham, had no merit, and was a malicious attempt by the competitor to remove him from the market.

The investors immediately withdrew from the process. Euro-Phoenix had no choice but to resign. The company did not achieve its financing, and eventually folded. Whatever you do, do not withhold information from your advisors.

advisor can help you present that information in the best possible light to investors, if that is the appropriate response. Or if the worst comes to the worst, your advisor may advise you to not take your business to market until the problem in question has been rectified.

> If you withhold information from investors, and they become aware of this during Due Diligence, the ramifications could be severe.

If you withhold information from investors, and they become aware of this during Due Diligence, the ramifications could be severe. They may decide to walk away from the deal altogether and possibly even claim for damages. Or they may instruct their legal advisors to draft a much more comprehensive set of **Representations and Warranties** in the **Sale and Purchase Agreement (SPA)** than might otherwise have been required. It's better to talk it over with your advisors.

Risks come in all shapes and sizes. To give you an idea of what they might look like, let's look at a random and incomplete list of some of the types of risk your company may face:

- *Client risks:* Is your client list well diversified, or does one client represent a dominant volume of your revenues or profitability? What are the chances of losing your most profitable client(s) (see Box 5.8)?
- *Technological or industry risks:* What are the chances of your company being left behind by technological change? What other industry-related risks are there? Some businesses need to reinvent themselves (e.g., change their business models) every few years.
- *Competitive risks:* What is the probability of competition intensifying, whether through new players entering your market, or existing players intensifying the competition?
- *Human resources risks:* What are the chances of losing some of your key staff? How difficult would it be to replace them? What are the chances of these staff members going into competition with your firm and taking away some of your business? Does your firm have an ample supply of blue-collar labor? Has the cost of staff been escalating rapidly? Could it escalate rapidly in the future? Do you have one or more unions covering the labor pool? What risks might this entail? Do you have unfunded pension obligations? Do staff members have stock options that might have an acceleration clause regarding certain events (i.e., their bonus may come due if there is a change of control or liquidity

event in the company)? In the event of a change of control, would your company be liable for any extraordinary severance payments? Has the company regularly paid its social security and payroll taxes (see Box 5.9)? If management receives a big payout under a liquidity event, is there a chance of diminished motivation?

- *Supply risks:* Does your company have an ample supply of all the raw materials and other inputs it needs to carry on business? What are the chances of disruption in this supply?
- *Regulatory risks:* What are the chances of laws or regulations changing in a way that could adversely affect your company? Are there any ambiguities in laws or regulations that could be construed by government authorities or third parties against your company?
- *Environmental risks:* Has there been any water, air, or land pollution associated with your products or on the property used or owned by your company? An increasing number of legal jurisdictions have strict liability provisions, which don't ask questions about how the pollution was caused: if the pollution is on your land, you may be liable for remediation, even if you did not cause it.
- *Financial risks:* How high is the company's leverage and what are the chances of default? If your company is listed on a stock exchange, are there chances of a hostile takeover? What are the possible effects of currency exchange rate fluctuations on the profitability of your company? In the event of a change of control, what rights do the company's banks or financiers have? What is the risk that your financial statements are misstated?
- *Product liability risks:* What are the chances of your products needing to be recalled, repaired, or replaced? Similarly, if your business is in an advisory business, what is the potential downside from errors or omissions?
- *Intellectual property risks:* Does your company have good and valid rights to intellectual property? Does it own patents or trademarks, for example? When do these expire?

This list is nowhere near exhaustive. I could go on for pages and pages. I just want to give you a taste of the types of risk you should be looking for. You may be aware that there is a direct link between risk and reward. This is a basic principle of corporate finance.

One of the reasons that there is often a price gap between buyers and sellers of businesses is that the sellers may be much more comfortable or used to dealing with the risks in the business than the buyers. Similarly, different investors will have different perceptions of the risks involved in your business, which similarly explains why different investors may give differing valuations of your company. These different perceptions of risk flow through to valuation.

One of the reasons that owners frequently ask too much for their businesses is that they don't appreciate the level of risk inherent in their company. As mentioned, the perceptions of different investors will vary, which partially explains why different investors may offer different prices for your business. As a business owner, you need to understand that the investor who does not know your company, potentially not even your industry or your country of operation, will need to develop a level of comfort with the risks involved. The IM and Due Diligence should help with this.

> Once you have identified the different types of risk, you should also develop a strategy for dealing with each of them.

The higher the perceived risk, the higher the cost of capital (**Weighted Average Cost of Capital: WACC**) investors will apply to your business, and the lower the price they will be prepared to offer (see the section on Valuation). So, as the business owner, you will need to take a direct interest in addressing issues of risk as early as possible, well before exit. Do not wait until you try to sell your business to implement these principles of risk management: the earlier you implement them the better. Once you have identified the different types of risk, you should also develop a strategy for dealing with each of them.

- *Insurance:* You might take out insurance to cover certain types of risk, such as product liability risks. If you own a service company, you might insure against errors and omissions.
- *Matching of currencies:* You could try offsetting sales in a certain currency by purchasing materials or inputs in that currency. If that doesn't work, hedging might provide a solution.
- *Renegotiating contracts:* Human resources risks may sometimes be mitigated by renegotiating contracts (to contain non-compete agreements, etc.).
- *Diversifying:* Client risks may be mitigated by diversifying your business to more clients.

Of course, you will need to make a cost/benefit analysis for each decision: is it worth the cost and effort of implementing the solution? Remember, the decision should be analyzed not only from your perspective, but also from an investor's perspective. If you really feel strongly about implementing a particular solution, it will still have been worth your while to investigate the costs and benefits. You could, of course, wait and see if the investor really insists on it, and if he or she does, you might say: "Well, it is possible to hedge this particular foreign exchange exposure, but it will cost you $250,000 a year. Do you think it's worth it?" If they say yes, the chances are that they will argue that this is a legitimate cost of carrying on business, hence depressing the profitability, cash flow, and the valuation of your business. Box 5.11 refers to an instance where the sellers did nothing to prepare themselves from a risk management view; they did not even retain advisors!

> Don't assume that problems can always be resolved as they arise during Due Diligence.

## OPERATIONAL IMPROVEMENTS TO THE BUSINESS

> Owners should be overwhelmed by the number of potential ways in which they could improve their business. The trick is to prioritize and focus on those that are most crucial.

I am convinced that it is always possible to do better when operating a business. As a business owner/manager myself, I believe owners should be overwhelmed by the number of potential ways in which they could improve their businesses. The trick is to prioritize and focus on those that are most crucial. If you are considering selling your business or raising financing in the coming years, get an investor's perspective on your business as to what operational improvements might be advisable. Here are just a few examples:

### Begin Strengthening Key Staff

You are in the strongest position vis-à-vis investors if you can show a functional organization chart and full management team, capable of managing the company and insuring its growth even in the absence of the owner/manager.

Cast your mind back to what we discussed earlier about corporate governance issues. Now consider the following steps in light of that discussion:

## BOX 5.11    INVESTOR CONDUCTING DUE DILIGENCE OF A SERVICES COMPANY

An investor was investigating the feasibility of purchasing a particular service company. My firm was retained by a French investor as the financial advisor; the investor also retained legal and accounting advisors.

After approximately three weeks, the audit and legal advisors reported their findings to the head office in Paris (without the courtesy of a prior consultation with us, the financial advisors). They painted a picture of doom and gloom regarding the nature of the client contracts. In a nutshell, the reversion of ownership of leased equipment from the services company to its ultimate client brought into question the legitimacy of certain deductions under tax legislation with respect to sophisticated leasing arrangements.

Was the potential exposure large? YES

What was the chance of the tax authority ever making an issue of the problem? LOW

Was the problem manageable or curable? YES

The problem was that the audit and legal advisors only dealt with the first of these issues. They sounded the alarm bell in the Paris head office at the most senior levels of the firm, so that no amount of explanation on our part could explain that the problem was manageable. Management had made up its mind and the damage was done. Our client decided to back away from the Transaction.

The point is that by doing a little advance preparation and reviewing the contracts prior to introducing the company to investors, the sellers could have identified this issue and renegotiated a number of contracts with their clients. Problem solved. Don't assume that problems can always be resolved as they arise during Due Diligence.

Several years later, the same services company approached us to represent it and sell the company. We helped it solve the problem, and within 10 months of receiving the mandate had successfully sold the company.

This anecdote also illustrates the tendency of certain legal and audit firms to take a cautious approach. Some advisors are better at sounding the alarm than prescribing constructive solutions and managing risks. In this day and age of mass litigation, it is not necessarily in their interests to go out on a limb; sometimes it's easier just to sound the alarm.

---

### BOX 5.12    AN AGRICULTURAL PROCESSING COMPANY

An agricultural processing company had a CEO who reported to a Managing Director, who in return reported to a Chairman. The company didn't have a sales or marketing department. The three gentlemen performed this function between them.

It was an easy recommendation: to have one CEO, who would report to a Chairman of an active Board. And the newly created position of Commercial Officer, in charge of sales and marketing, should report to the CEO.

---

- *CEO or COO:* Is there anyone in your company who deserves to be promoted to CEO, in which case you might become chairperson? This might be an option worth considering, particularly if you are not intent on staying for a longer post-purchase transition period. If that does not work, you might consider appointing someone as Chief Operating Officer.
- *Sales and marketing:* This is an area at which investors will look very closely, particularly in the context of a one-man show. Do you, as the owner/manager, carry the company from a sales and marketing perspective? In other words, if the investor buys your business, how easy or difficult will it be for him or her to continue to grow or even to ignite growth in the company? Investors fear that the loyalty of the clients is not to the business, but to the owner, and that once the owner leaves, this loyalty will disappear, too. A good way to solve this issue is to create strong, independent sales and marketing departments within your company (Box 5.12).
- *Key staff should be locked in:* There are many ways of locking in key staff. Consider giving them equity, options, or phantom equity—performance bonuses or bonuses for loyalty. The effect of key staff leaving during the sale process can be quite devastating and destructive to the value of your company. Think of the business relationships, know-how, and so on, that key staff members can take with them, and how long it might take to recruit and train a new employee. Pension plans, medical benefits, or other benefits might also help lock in key staff. In addition to using carrots, you might also consider using the stick: insist on a non-compete clause in their agreements.

Questions of strengthening staff must, of course, be viewed in light of their potentially augmenting expenses and diminishing the cash flow and profitability of the firm. Sometimes individuals may be promoted from within the firm at relatively modest marginal cost, without augmenting head count. On other occasions, when hiring staff from the outside particularly, this type of change may involve major investments. Staffing changes are ideally done well before you go to market, so that the individuals will have proven themselves, and presumably generated more than enough benefit for the firm to cover their expenses. Investors prefer dealing with proven rather than unproven staff.

## Cost Reductions

I fully realize that I am giving contradictory advice in saying that you should consider strengthening your management team, while reducing costs. This is one of the tensions inherent in any business. It is also the reason that scale is important: larger companies can afford better management.

Look at your own costs versus industry standards.

> If your competitors are operating at costs below your operating costs, chances are that you could learn something from them.

Benchmarking costs as a percentage of revenues is a particularly useful analysis. If your competitors are operating at costs below your operating costs, chances are that you could learn something from them. Either your competitor is smarter than you are in keeping costs down, or your competitor is sacrificing quality (see Box 5.13).

---

### BOX 5.13    A CEMENT COMPANY

A multinational cement company with offices in more than 40 countries was operating at considerably higher costs than the corporate average in one particular country. Our role, as advisor, was to find the cost discrepancies and design a strategy for reducing them (around €5 million). We then helped the company successfully execute the strategy.

## Other Operating Improvements

Benchmarking can also help reveal whether your business is settling payables or collecting receivables at a slower or faster rate than the industry average. Similarly, it can help determine whether your inventory turns are faster or slower than the industry average.

These are usually items that are quite easy to implement; they are the low-lying fruit that should be picked before you take your company to market. Think of it this way: investors will be assessing your company based on the quality of its management. If the management is unable to pick the low-lying fruit, it does not bode well for solving more complex management issues.

There are almost an infinite number of ways to improve your business operationally, including the following suggestions.

*Reduction of costs of production and lead times via:*
- process re-engineering,
- updating technology or equipment,
- IT improvements,
- improving procurement.

*Reducing the capital deployed in your business (and therefore improving the efficiency of the remaining capital deployed) via:*
- selling off non core assets,
- selling off dead inventory,
- reducing receivables, and so on.

The above points should be considered as illustrations, not a comprehensive checklist.


## NON-ARM'S-LENGTH SITUATIONS

Let's assume that you own two or more companies, but only want to sell one of them. Investors will scrutinize such situations carefully. Their first question will be: If you sell the company in question, will you be available to assist with the transition, or will you be much more focused on running the other business in which you retain direct ownership? Even if you tell the investor that you would spend 50 percent of your time over a specified number of months assisting with the transition, this will be difficult for the investor to verify.

In addition, non-arm's-length situations can lead to a number of complications:

- Where there have been non-arm's-length Transactions between affiliated companies (e.g., where you as the owner might have an interest in several companies), have these Transactions been at market prices, or at a price that might inflate the profitability of the company being sold?
- There may also be liabilities due to the tax authorities if pricing has not been on commercial terms, and if there is insufficient documentation backing up the claim that Transactions were on commercial terms.
- Where two or more companies are sharing resources (e.g., IT infrastructure, financial department, HR function, and real estate), it becomes tricky to allocate the appropriate level of expense to each of the companies.
- If the company being sold has been piggy-backing on the infrastructure of a non-arm's-length company, it may be necessary to replace that infrastructure in the company being sold (e.g., accounting department, IT infrastructure, etc.)
- Management fees may compensate for services necessary for the ongoing functioning of the company, or they may just be a way to siphon money out of the company in question. Questions raised might include: how do you find substitute services at an affordable price? Could there be tax liabilities?

These types of non-arm's-length issues are seldom fatal to a Transaction if both buyer and seller have a strong desire to complete the deal, and the seller provides full disclosure, although the complications and delays in negotiating and closing Transactions may be considerable. If possible, try to extricate your company from all non-arm's-length Transactions for at least one audited financial year prior to taking your company to market. This will help remove any doubt about possible manipulation of profitability.

# CHAPTER 6

# Business Plan and Valuation

*Value is what people are willing to pay for it.*
—John Naisbitt (b. 1929)
American author and public speaker

This chapter is not designed to make you an expert in building business plans or performing a valuation. It is rather intended to provide business owners with an overview of what you need to know about these subjects prior to an exit or **Transaction**. The chapter will be broken down into the following sections:

- reasons for making a Business Plan
- should you perform a valuation?
- recasting financial statements (e.g., so as to remove possible distortions)
- building a Business Plan
- an introduction to valuation
- types of valuation (**Discounted Cash Flow (DCF)**, comparables, and others)
- adjustments to valuation (synergies, cash or noncore assets, etc.)

The Business Plan and valuation are integral parts of **Business Exit Planning**. The aforementioned knowledge should help business owners hire and supervise a team and ask better questions.

## REASONS FOR MAKING A BUSINESS PLAN

The absence of a Business Plan is simply bad management practice.

Every company should have a Business Plan going forward for at least two to three years; the absence of a Business Plan is simply bad management practice. Chances are that most investors will think the same way. If you are thinking of performing a DCF valuation, you should also extend that Business Plan to cover at least four to five years of forward statements or to whenever you expect operating cash flows to stabilize.

A Business Plan helps you in numerous respects:

- It establishes a prognosis for growth of the company, and may analyze several scenarios for growth (or contraction).
- Under the prognosis, or for different scenarios, it will tell you whether you have insufficient internal financing (a financing gap) and need to look for additional outside funding.
- It may serve as a useful tool for setting targets for management under various types of bonus plans, or budgets for various managers within the organization.
- It allows management to engage in sensitivity analysis, that is, to analyze various what-if scenarios. For example, what if we were to expand the plant by so many tons per year? What if we were to establish a new sales office? What if we were to purchase a major new piece of equipment? Given the assumptions behind the decision, the Business Plan would calculate whether the decision enhances profitability and cash flow. It would also help you ascertain whether the required hurdle rate for the **Internal Rate of Return (IRR)** can be achieved.
- It will also let you calculate the IRR in your business. A financial investor, such as a private equity fund, will generally want to see an IRR of approximately 20 to 30 percent (denominated in euro or USD). Unless you have a Business Plan and can perform this calculation, your attempt to sell to a financial investor will be little more than a stab in the dark.
- Many investors will insist on seeing your Business Plan, or at least the highlights from it, so have it ready!

> A Business Plan is a very good idea, even if you are not planning on selling your business to an investor.

While many business owner/managers have an excellent sense of intuition and are able to navigate quite well by instinct, a Business Plan sometimes forecasts some unexpected results. For example, it is surprising how much cash a business can throw off during a recessionary cycle, particularly when it ties up fewer resources in funding inventory or receivables. It comes as even more of a surprise to some business owners that when a business turns the corner, and sales are climbing nicely again, the financing gap may widen unexpectedly because the business experienced a loss in cash reserves during the down cycle, while the up cycle will tie up tremendous amounts of cash to finance the rebuilding of receivables and inventory. In a nutshell, a Business Plan is a very good idea, even if you are not planning an exit.

## SHOULD YOU PERFORM A VALUATION OF YOUR BUSINESS?

There are many reasons for performing a valuation in the context of Business Exit Planning or selling your business. The reasons for not doing so are few and weak! Reasons in favor include:

- *A benchmark against which to measure offers:* If you receive one or more offers for your business, how will you know whether those offers are good, excellent, or downright poor, unless you have performed some analysis and a valuation of your own? A valuation allows you to put any offers you may receive into the proper context.
- *Information to support your negotiations:* If an investor tells you that last year, there was a business in the same sector that sold for very low multiples, and that he or she thinks that this should be the basis for valuing your own business, what can you do? With a valuation, you might be able to answer that there was another business that sold this year at much higher multiples, and because this business is more comparable, this is the business that should provide the basis for valuation. Or you might provide 10 comparable Transactions, with the average and median multiples.
- *Helps you resist attempts to reduce the price:* The investor is almost sure, at some point during the negotiations, to raise certain aspects about your business in an effort to reduce the price. This could be anything from the loss of a contract to unfavorable currency fluctuations. Unless you have a business model, it will be very difficult, perhaps impossible, to quantify the potential loss in value. Similarly, it may be difficult to quantify whether other favorable developments may have occurred, developments which might more than offset the negatives.

As a colleague of mine likes to say, there is no such thing as a good company or a bad company, only a good valuation or a bad valuation.

## RECASTING FINANCIAL STATEMENTS

Owners and managers of businesses, as well as financial advisors, like to talk about business being worth a certain multiple of Earnings Before Interest, Taxes, Depreciation, and Amortization (EBITDA) (e.g., six times EBITDA), or a certain multiple of Earnings Before Interest and Tax (EBIT). One of the most frequent errors in performing this kind of analysis is to take the EBITDA or EBIT numbers at face value, without considering whether these numbers really reflect the true economic performance of your company.

> Your financial statements will seldom reflect the real economic performance of your company.

Your financial statements will seldom reflect the real economic performance of your company. Numerous distortions may creep in, such as:

- charitable donations
- perks (club memberships, etc.)
- insurance (if there is too much or not enough insurance)
- maintenance (e.g., where it has been deferred)

In such instances, it is good practice to adjust the financial statements of the company to reflect true economic performance. Let's have a look at three different examples:

1. The owner/manager of Company A draws no salary from the company. His market salary would be $200,000 per year, or $250,000 grossed up with all payroll and social security taxes. If an investor were to buy this business, the former owner/manager would presumably not be prepared to stay and work for free indefinitely; nor would a replacement be willing to work for free. Presumably the new manager would ask for a market salary. Hence EBITDA and EBIT would be diminished by $250,000.
2. The son of the owner/manager of Company B is 17 years old and is working part-time for Company B, drawing a salary of $100,000 (fully grossed up). The son is not producing anything of value for Company B, nor would the investor wish to continue with the son on the payroll. In this case, EBITDA and EBIT would be increased by $100,000.

3. The owner of Company C purchased four helicopters. This was not at all necessary for operation of the company's core business. (This has actually happened!) The $450,000 required for the operation of the helicopters should be added back to EBITDA and EBIT.

Interestingly, when Company C sold the four helicopters, it received a capital gain of $375,000. When EBIT and EBITDA are calculated, they should not include nonrecurring gains or losses on Transactions (e.g., disposal of non-core assets).

Note, too, that with respect to Company C, non-core assets such as the four helicopters should be valued separately and added to the valuation numbers that arise as a result of these operating profit multiples. The operating multiples should reflect the underlying financial performance of the core business (including only its core assets).

> My hair literally stands on end when financial advisors or business owners bandy about EBITDA or EBIT multiples, given the potential for inaccuracy.

My hair literally stands on end when financial advisors or business owners bandy about EBITDA or EBIT multiples, given the potential for inaccuracy. The problem is that if you're talking, for example, about a six times multiple, you are exaggerating the inaccuracy of the valuation by a factor of six as well! It's scary stuff. For example, if you had initially valued Company A prior to recasting at $3 million (six times EBITDA of $500,000), recasting would reduce EBITDA to $250,000, and hence the valuation from $3 million to $1.5 million. This is enough to keep anyone awake at night.

Comparables are often calculated for the current year, the past year, and sometimes as a forecast for the coming year. But you have to remember to apply the recasting to *all* years where comparable analysis is performed. Similarly, recasting should also be applied to the base year used in DCF analysis. The base year—that is, the most recent full year of performance that is used for projecting forward—should be adjusted for distortions.

Whenever you recast, don't forget to keep a copy of a memorandum reconciling your financial statements with your recast financial statements. Your investors will definitely want to understand the reconciliation. In the months that pass between preparing recast statements and the **Due Diligence** by investors, there may be a tendency to forget exactly how the recasting was conducted.

## BUILDING A BUSINESS PLAN

I'm not going to teach you how build a Business Plan—there are entire courses given on that particular subject—but rather provide you with a few insights into the context of Business Exit Planning to help ensure that your Business Plan is progressing in the right direction:

- *The base year should be free of distortions:* The base year may require recasting to ensure proper reflection of the economic performance of the firm.
- *Revenues should be segmented according to type:* Don't lump all revenues together. This is especially important because the investor will want to understand how you forecast revenue growth for each type of revenue.
- *Examine variations of your basic scenario:* Whereas your basic scenario might deal with what you consider to be your likeliest scenario, you should also develop an optimistic scenario and a pessimistic one. This will test your assumptions and provide a great deal of information about a wide range of topics, ranging from cash adequacy to the IRR.
- *Thoroughly document your assumptions:* When I first began to build computer programs, I discovered the abbreviation GIGO: Garbage In Garbage Out. The same principle applies to building business models. The quality of the model is only as good as the quality of information loaded into the model. The documentation of assumptions is often much more extensive than the model itself. For instance:
  - What is the projected inflation rate, or is the model in real currency?
  - What is the basis for forecasting each source of revenue?
  - What is the basis for forecasting costs (a percentage of revenue, fixed costs subject to inflation, or something else)?
  - What are the assumptions behind capital expenditure over the coming years?
  - What will be required to maintain equipment and premises?
  - What is the useful life of the equipment? When will it require replacement?
  - At what rate are salaries expected to increase? What evidence is this estimate based on?
  - What are your assumptions with respect to currency fluctuations?
  - What are your assumptions about inventory, accounts payable, and accounts receivable?
  - What are your assumptions with respect to debt financing (e.g., if you have variable-rate bank financing)?

> Testing the positive and negative variations of your assumptions in your scenario analysis is another extremely valuable management tool.

Documenting these assumptions is vital, because a change in any one of them will likely change the estimated value of your company. If the value parameters are not defined, the valuation may lack meaning. Testing the positive and negative variations of your assumptions in your scenario analysis is another extremely valuable management tool.

Anyone reading your Business Plan should be able to understand the spreadsheet and assumptions without asking questions. If they have to ask questions, you have either left something out, or you haven't been clear about your model or explanations. I have seen Business Plans where the assumptions were documented alright…but lacked supporting evidence. It is far better to provide the supporting evidence as well (source of inflation forecast, market research supporting revenue growth, etc.).

Are you familiar with hockey stick Business Plans? Plans in which, say, three or four years down the road, revenues, cash flow, and profitability suddenly begin curving upwards, often without persuasive supporting rationale. Hockey stick Business Plans are likely to be counterproductive, in that they diminish, rather than augment, the credibility of revenue and cash flow projections, which ultimately underpin the value of the firm.

## INTRODUCTORY COMMENTS ON VALUATION

My son once had a biking accident. The clinic x-rayed his jaw from several different angles to see if it could find even a hairline crack in his bones. In the same way, the use of multiple types of valuation methodologies can help confirm valuations. It's better to get the valuation from different angles. Differences in results among different types of valuations may raise some interesting questions about the assumptions going into the analysis; for example, whether the comparables were truly comparable, or whether the cash flow forecast may have been too optimistic (see Box 6.1).

> While a large body of theoretical knowledge is required to be a good business valuator, ultimately, good valuation requires good professional judgment.

---

### BOX 6.1   A FOOD INDUSTRY VALUATION

The parent company of a local food producer retained Euro-Phoenix to value its subsidiary. When it did not like the valuation we produced, it had a major global investment banking firm try to intimidate us into giving a higher valuation. It subsequently provided us with a Business Plan that bore no resemblance to any results that the company had produced in the past, and asked that the valuation be based on the Business Plan.

Fortunately, our mandate specified that our valuation was to be on the principles of fair market value, so we stuck to our guns. A year later, we learned that the parent company had been sold. It had been concerned about the lack of value of the local producer, and had tried to bolster that value with a valuation. As it turned out, the new owner of the parent company sold the local producer to local management for a nugatory amount.

---

There is no single magic formula for performing valuations. While a large body of theoretical knowledge is required to be a good business valuator, ultimately, good valuation requires good professional judgment. Even choosing the valuation methodology or methodologies to be used, as well as their relative weighting, is a matter of judgment.

Two of the most common methods for valuing companies while considering exit options are the DCF method and the comparables method. Both methods of valuation are designed to estimate the fair market value of a company.

The American Society of Appraisers defines fair market value as:

*The price, expressed in terms of cash equivalents, at which property would change hands between a hypothetical willing and able buyer and a hypothetical willing and able seller acting at arm's length in an open and unrestricted market, when neither is under compulsion to buy or sell and when both have reasonable knowledge of the relevant facts.*[1]

The actual price paid in a Transaction may differ from fair market value, due to factors such as:

- The motivation of the parties.
- The negotiation skills of the parties.
- The financial structure of the Transaction.

As the value of a business may fluctuate from day to day, it is important to agree with your business valuator on an effective date of valuation. Year-end is a convenient time, as you will usually have comprehensive audited financial statements for the year in question and for each of the preceding years.

## TYPES OF VALUATION

### Discounted Cash Flow Analysis

DCF valuation is based on the proposition that a company's value is based primarily on its future performance, not past or present financial indicators. That does not mean that the past or the present is irrelevant: we extrapolate the future from trends that evolve from the past to the present. What ultimately interests investors, however, is whether free cash flow is sustainable or whether it can be grown, and if so, with what degree of risk. As a business owner, you will need to understand certain principles to help you oversee the work of whoever is performing your DCF.

The essence of a DCF analysis is that it values the future cash flows of your business from the coming year until infinity. Given that $1 today is worth more than $1 tomorrow, there is a discount rate applied to the future cash flows that brings them back to a present value. The discount rate— **Working Average Cost of Capital (WACC)** —is a blended cost of debt and equity, adjusted for the appropriate level of risk for your company (the higher the risk, the higher the return expected, hence the higher the WACC and the lower the valuation of the company). DCF is very sensitive to WACC, so it is important to get the WACC calculation right. There is also a degree of subjectivity in developing WACC (particularly estimating the cost of equity and the appropriate mix of debt and equity), which, once again, requires professional judgment.

The cash flows from the coming year to infinity are typically broken down into two components. During an initial period of four to seven years (known as the Explicit Period), the DCF calculation relies on the free cash flows derived from your Business Plan, and discounts them year-to-year to a present value (once again, using WACC). With respect to the time horizon beyond the Business Plan (known as the Residual Period), the assumption is that the free cash flow has stabilized, and the sum of free cash flows during the Residual Period discounted to the present value is known as the Terminal Value. The value of the company is the sum of these two components. If the Terminal Value constitutes more than 60 to 70 percent of the value of your business, then you should be suspicious. It is probably symptomatic of a hockey stick approach.

The comparables and DCF analyses are likely to produce what is known as an Enterprise Value. By subtracting debt, you arrive at an Equity Value, that is, the value that you, as a business owner, may be expected to realize from the sale of your shares. Don't forget, though, that from equity value (assuming you achieve the valuation in a Transaction) you will still need to pay taxes (such as capital gains taxes) and advisory fees.

When your financial team has prepared the Business Plan and valuation, go through it with a fine-tooth comb. It should be presented in layman's language. Test the assumptions. Are they reasonable? Are they well documented?

## Comparables Analysis

Comparables analysis derives the value of your company based on a comparison with comparable companies. There are generally two types of comparables analysis:

1. *Sales of private companies:* If you have a company in the electrical wholesaling business, for example, comparables analysis would find those mergers and acquisitions (M&A) Transactions of comparable companies in the same business over the past few years, and analyze the relevant multiples (primarily revenue, EBITDA, and EBIT). The universe of companies used as a peer group requires careful selection. The companies should come from a similar economic environment as the company being valued (similar macroeconomic factors, growth prospects, etc.). The advantage of this method of comparables analysis is that it examines valuations of Transactions of privately held companies, ideally of a similar size range and geographic scope to your own company. The disadvantage is that the Transactions are from the past, so the comparables are not fully current. Any change in market conditions will therefore not be reflected in the analysis. For example, if there has been a recent collapse of equity valuations (e.g., on stock exchanges), this method should not be relied upon too heavily.

2. *Publicly listed companies:* This method of comparables analysis compares the value of your company to publicly listed companies that are in a similar sector and, if possible, similar geographic area (once again, by comparing multiples such as revenues, EBITDA, and EBIT). The advantage of this type of valuation is that equity valuations of publicly listed companies are completely up to date. You can get the most recent quote from the stock exchange. The disadvantage is that public companies are usually much larger than privately owned companies. They are not comparable in a number of respects. For example, publicly

listed companies generally have much better corporate governance than privately held companies. They generally have far greater depth of management, a working Board of Directors, extensive disclosure, quarterly reports, and so on. Hence, public companies typically trade at a substantial premium compared to smaller, privately held companies. There might be a number of different premiums and discounts applied in the context of arriving at a valuation. Once again, excellent professional judgment is required.

## Other Types of Valuation Methodologies

Some of the valuation methodologies worth keeping in mind are:

- *Net asset value:* Net asset value typically takes all of the major assets and liabilities of a company and adjusts their value to fair market value (e.g., as opposed to book value or historical cost) as of a particular valuation date. This valuation methodology is not suitable for companies that have substantial assets of an intangible nature, and is only used in very limited circumstances. The method may be appropriate where a company has low operating cash flows, and where liquidation may be an option in the future. It may also be used for valuing holding companies that own various shares and assets. The method is probably not applicable to valuing the interest of a minority shareholder, as a minority shareholder does not control the process of disposition of the various assets. Investors might also use this valuation method if a one-man show is exiting the business and they don't anticipate the company continuing as a going concern in his absence.
- *Brand (or intangible) value:* There may also be elements of value in a company such as brand or other intellectual property or intangibles. It is a very delicate question whether brand or intellectual property should be valued separately from or in addition to the value of a company. The Coca Cola brand, for example, may be worth tens of billions; but that value should already be reflected in the cash flow generating capacity of the company and cannot be sold separately. A good brand, however, may have a considerable synergistic value for an investor, who might be able to do far more with the brand than the company that currently owns the brand (e.g., international roll out of the brand).
- *Value of tax-loss carryforwards:* Some companies, which are not even going concerns, are sold for their value attributable to tax-loss carryforwards. When a profitable company merges with a company with tax-loss carryforwards, tax legislation may permit the deduction of the past losses from the present or future profits of the merged entity. Does

your company have tax-loss carryforwards? These may have value if (a) they are transferrable under the laws of your country; (b) the acquirer would be prepared to merge with your company (e.g., the company has emerged perfectly clean from a Due Diligence); and (c) the laws of your country would permit the merged company to deduct the accumulated losses. Where tax-loss carryforwards are allowed, they must typically be used within a certain time period, or they will expire. A buyer is typically willing to pay a fraction of the benefit that he or she derives from the tax-loss carryforwards.

## ADJUSTMENTS TO VALUATIONS

Fair market value describes what a company will sell for in an arm's length Transaction. It values a company on a standalone basis; that is, it does not take into account possible synergies that might be experienced by an investor or merger partner. This is not surprising, given that in a pre-Transaction valuation, the company has not yet been put up for sale, and an investor has probably not even been identified. There are a number of adjustments made to standalone value.

### Strategic or Synergistic Value

Synergy might be defined as 1 + 1 = 3; in the context of buying companies, where you put two companies together, the combined unit may be worth more than the sum of its parts.

Take the example of an acquiring company with an EBITDA of $2 million per annum and an acquired company with an EBITDA of $1 million per annum, but whose combined entity could produce a $4 million per annum EBITDA. Assuming that the standard industry valuations were in the range of six times EBITDA, if the investor paid $9 million for the target company, it would still create $3 million of shareholder value for the shareholders of the investor company (even though it is technically paying a handsome nine times EBITDA to the shareholders of the acquired entity!). You have to be very careful with synergy analysis, as a failure to deliver the synergies will then dilute shareholder value for the shareholders of the acquiring company.

A company may have a strategic or synergistic value well beyond its standalone value.

---

### BOX 6.2    TELECOMMUNICATIONS CONSOLIDATION

In a country of 60 million inhabitants, there were eight telecom providers. Each of them had been trying to acquire the others for almost a decade. The first deal that was struck was for a whopping *four times* the standalone value of the target company. This valuation was justified by the fact that the acquisition would give the acquirer the so-called first-mover advantage. Nevertheless, prior to the closing of the Transaction, the acquirer itself went through a change of control, and the deal fell apart.

---

Strategic value occurs when a company has value to an investor for strategic reasons (e.g., the company controls a particular technology or market segment). This explains why high-tech investors are sometimes prepared to pay stratospheric prices for companies that have barely started producing revenue. A company may have a strategic or synergistic value well beyond its standalone value. This may be the case where market consolidation in a particular country or region is just beginning. The first company to make an acquisition is then perceived as having momentum and may be willing to pay a substantial premium over the standalone value, to provide it with such momentum (see Box 6.2). Conversely, the last company in a particular sector to be consolidated may have significantly less appeal for investors, and so may trade at a discount. This is all the more reason that good business judgment is so important in valuations.

Investors typically allow for five types of synergy calculations:[2]

- *Cost savings:* Generally easy to quantify, and include elimination of duplication in plants, equipment, staff, and so on.
- *Revenue enhancement:* Much more difficult to quantify, and more frequently a source of error. For example, when ABN merged with AMRO, it became a player in the syndicated loan business, which neither company was previously in a position to access.
- *Process improvements:* This includes adopting best practices and core competencies that are stronger in one company into the other company.
- *Financial engineering:* For example, if a multinational company acquires your company, chances are that it has much cheaper access to debt, and can refinance your debt at lower interest costs.

■ *Tax benefits:* These may include absorbing tax-loss carryforwards, restructuring debt into higher tax locations, and restructuring purchasing or other shared services or administrative functions into low-tax jurisdictions.

> There is no guarantee that the merging of two companies will produce synergies.

The main reason that bid processes are competitive, with no asking price, is to provide maximum encouragement to bidders to share the synergy value with the vendor. Once you are in exclusive negotiations with one investor, he or she may have little incentive to acknowledge synergy values. Also, the concept of negative synergy should be borne in mind (e.g., when $2 + 2 = 3$). There is no guarantee that the merging of two companies will produce synergies. If you merge a well-functioning company into an inefficient, poorly run company, for example, you may destroy value. Conglomerates often trade at a discount to the sum of the parts, because the market would actually prefer pure play investments in particular sectors, and investors pick and choose their own sector weighting, rather than let the managers of a conglomerate make such choices. Being part of a larger entity may add to the costs of administration, governance, and so on. A large number of bank acquisitions over the past decade have been value destructive, promoting diseconomies of scale. "Received wisdom has it that three-quarters of mergers fail to create shareholder value and half actually destroy it."[3]

## Control Premiums

A **Control Premium** is paid where the purchase of shares allows the investor to exercise control over the company; that is, make decisions, such as appointing management, approving the business plan, raising capital, and so on. If an investor purchases 51 percent of a company, that 51 percent will generally bear the right to make decisions regarding the governance of the company. The price per share of that 51 percent therefore may be considerably higher than the price per share of the remaining 49 percent. Control premiums may vary from negligible to 50 percent or higher compared to the price of shares or quotas that do not exercise control. The extent of the premium may depend on numerous factors. For example, what governance rights do the minority shares have? These rights may be provided by law (e.g., in most countries there are minority shareholder protection rights, which will give rights to prevent dilution, or other rights) or by way of a **Shareholders' Agreement,** in addition to those rights provided by law (such rights might include the rights to veto certain types of decisions, such as appointment of new management, the Business Plan or Strategy of the company, etc.). In general, the more rights obtained by the minority shareholders, the lower the Control Premium.

Sometimes, where companies are publicly traded and share ownership is fragmented, a Control Premium may be obtained when less than 50 percent of the shares are purchased.

## Cash and Non-Core Assets

DCF and comparables valuations typically assume that a business has sufficient cash to carry on the business. Where a company has large amounts of surplus cash, these may be declared as cash dividends from the company, and hence may be valued separately. Conversely, if a cash injection were required to realize the Business Plan, this would be subtracted from the value of the company. Often there will be a discussion between the buyer and seller as to what is a sufficient amount of cash for the business to carry in the normal course of operations. The area is somewhat subjective, and where the issue arises, it is likely to be the subject of a negotiation.

Where a business owns non-core assets (machinery, real estate, patents, etc.) that are not required for the company to produce its Business Plan (indeed, they often produce no revenue at all), the value of these assets may be added to the value of the company (or, alternatively, excluded from the scope of the business valuation). For example, if a service company owns real estate that it is not using in its core business, then either the scope of valuation of the service company should exclude the real estate, or the value of the service company as a going concern should be augmented by the fair market value of the real estate.

## Other Adjustments

The reliability of a valuation is directly proportionate to the level of effort expended on getting to know the company.

There may be many other adjustments to value that arise from Due Diligence (litigation against the company or even the threat of litigation, key staff leaving, tax liabilities, environmental liabilities, key contracts coming due sooner than expected, off-balance sheet liabilities, etc.). In a nutshell, the reliability of a valuation is directly proportionate to the level of effort expended on getting to know the company.

# CHAPTER 7

# Tax Planning, Estate Planning and Insurance

*"While we are postponing, life speeds by."*
—Seneca (3BC–65AD)

Tax planning, estate planning, and insurance are three subjects that are extremely important to **Business Exit Planning**; there is a limited amount one can say about each of them in a tome that is not tied to specific laws in a specific legal jurisdiction at a specific point in time. While I touch on a few general principles in each of these areas, I would urge the reader to explore these subjects further with local experts or other local sources.

## TAX PLANNING

As your objective is probably to maximize after-tax **Transaction** revenues rather than Transaction revenues, it is worthwhile paying attention to tax planning issues during the Business Exit Planning process.

Tax advisors also distinguish between *tax avoidance*, which means carefully studying the laws of one or more jurisdictions to legally minimize or avoid incidence of tax, and *tax evasion*, which involves non-payment of tax by breaking the law. As a business owner, you will need to decide for yourself the degree to which you engage in tax planning. There is a cost/ benefit involved, because advisory fees for tax avoidance may be expensive. There is always the risk that laws may change (e.g., to close loopholes) or that the tax authorities interpret the law differently than your tax advisors.

One of the more obvious dimensions of tax planning when exiting your Operating Company (Opco) is the treatment of capital gains taxes when you sell your business. In most tax jurisdictions, the sale of shares triggers a capital gains tax that can be quite substantial. If your Opco is owned by a Holding Company (Holdco) that is incorporated in a jurisdiction where there are no capital gains, however, you may be successful in avoiding capital gains tax altogether. Some of the issues which you will need to deal with under this kind of a solution might be:

- How do you transfer the shares of the Opco into the ownership of the Holdco? Had you thought many years ahead and put the Opco into the ownership of a Holdco when you founded the Opco, your chances of avoiding taxes would be higher.
- How do you get your money out of the Holdco after it has sold shares in Opco? This may well trigger tax, too.

In lieu of a share purchase, the investor may insist on an asset purchase. In this type of situation, tax planning may be even more complex, as there may be capital gains at the level of each piece of equipment, not to mention land and other assets. There could also be land-transfer taxes involved or value added tax (VAT) on equipment. The difference between the purchase price of assets and the book value of the assets is classified as goodwill in many jurisdictions. The treatment of goodwill, and its possible depreciation, under asset purchases is always a complex subject. (See Box 7.1 for an illustration of a Transaction structure that saved the parties to the Transaction tens of millions over what may have been achieved without tax planning.)

Another issue that is generally left until much too late is the deductibility of advisory fees and VAT or other taxes associated with advisory fees. For example, in most jurisdictions, you can only deduct VAT on advisory fees if there is a legal entity generating revenue that also brings in VAT, against which the VAT on advisory fees may be offset. For an individual shareholder, this is usually not the case. Given that on larger mid-sized Transactions, the VAT may easily be in the hundreds of thousands, this is an issue worth addressing early, rather than at the eleventh hour prior to closing the Transaction, when there is almost no room to maneuver.

## ESTATE PLANNING

There are at least as many people who hesitate or procrastinate with estate planning as with Business Exit Planning. This is not surprising, given that most people do not like to plan around their own mortality. Others believe that their family members or heirs will be able to sort things out. Estate

## BOX 7.1  A TELECOMMUNICATIONS COMPANY

Investors, represented by Euro-Phoenix, had negotiated for over a year with respect to a particular telecommunications company.

As the parties neared finalization of the SPA, it turned out that the seller had accumulated huge losses in its telecommunications company, which were actually substantially larger than the purchase price that our client was willing to pay for the company. The seller was completely unwilling to proceed with the Transaction unless it could trigger a tax loss on disposition. The seller's tax advisors advised it that the only way of triggering the tax loss was to liquidate the company. Our client, of course, was not willing to pay tens of millions of euro unless the subject of the purchase was a going concern.

What ensued is one of the more creative and complex tax-driven Transactions, known by tax advisors as a butterfly Transaction: The seller demerged the operating telecom company into two entities, Company A and Company B. Company A was liquidated, whereby the seller could trigger its tax liability. Our client then purchased the assets of Company A from a newly incorporated company, Company A1. With respect to Company B, which had all the client contracts of the old operating company, there was no liquidation; our client simply purchased the shares of Company B as a going concern, and then re-merged the assets of Company A1 with the shares of Company B.

The complexity of this Transaction added a further six months to the timeline, and was very expensive in terms of legal and tax advisory fees. Nevertheless, the seller received its desired tax loss, and our client, the buyer, shared some of those gains in the form of a purchase price that made the waiting, complexity, and additional fees worthwhile: a win-win solution for both. Tax planning can save millions of euro for both the buyer and seller of a business, although at the cost of some additional complexity and delay.

planning is about looking after your loved ones and the causes you believe in (e.g., via charitable donations). If you care about these, you should care enough to engage in estate planning. Wouldn't you rather plan for these than leave them to chance? Planning can reduce the potential for disputes. The structures you create in estate planning may also help you protect assets and weather an insolvency or breakdown of a marriage.

> A will is the cornerstone of your estate planning. It allows you to determine to whom your assets should be distributed and when.

A good place to start with estate planning is to make a list of all the assets you own, including your home, vehicles, bank accounts, company shares, and works of art. A detailed and accurate inventory will facilitate matters when the estate must be settled. Be careful to check the precise title to these assets. Do you own them personally, through a company, or share ownership with a family member? Whom would you want to end up owning the assets? Every country generally specifies a manner in which the assets of the deceased are distributed. Do you know how distribution would occur in your country? Is this the result you would want (and in the same ratios)? If not, you should consider writing a will, if you have not already done so. A will is the cornerstone of your estate planning. It allows you to determine to whom your assets should be distributed and when. If you don't leave a valid will, the laws of your country will regulate how your assets are distributed, which may be contrary to your preferences.

If there are estate taxes in your country, you would be well advised to ensure that the distribution of your estate happens tax efficiently (e.g., *legally avoiding*, rather than *illegally evading*, taxes). Possible strategies for avoiding tax might be providing gifts to your heirs while you are still alive or establishing a foundation or trust. Foundations or trusts can create great flexibility in terms of naming and subsequently changing beneficiaries, while allowing flexibility of timing of taxable income to beneficiaries. The importance of timing benefits should not be underestimated. For example, if you die intestate, your spouse and/or children may receive the estate, and they may immediately face a significant tax liability. If you establish a trust or foundation while you are alive, there is an excellent chance that you can avoid estate taxes; the funds can compound or accumulate tax free; and your children or grandchildren may receive the funds when they need them most and are in low tax brackets (e.g., when they are attending university).

Most jurisdictions with inheritance taxes also allow for a certain amount of assets to pass exempt from any estate taxes. Try to make maximum benefit of these exemptions. They may significantly reduce or entirely eliminate the need to pay estate tax.

A will may also be used as an instrument to appoint someone to handle your business affairs, to oversee the running of your company, etc., thus ensuring business continuity.

## Estate Planning in the Context of Business Exit Planning

So, you might ask, why are we talking about estate planning in the context of a discussion on Business Exit Planning? There are several reasons:

- The closing of a Transaction usually marks the freeing up of a substantial amount of cash. The larger the amount, the more incentive there is to ensure proper planning and use of funds.
- If, as a business owner, you are exiting in the context of preparing for retirement, you're probably at that stage in life where estate planning is appropriate.
- With a large amount of cash arising from a Transaction, it is generally worth considering the creation of structures that will allow you to shelter your investment income, at least the portion destined for inheritance.
- Minimizing the number of Transactions also helps to minimize tax. In most countries, each time you transfer ownership of shares and assets, you run the risk of triggering capital gains or other taxes. Hence, the Transaction of exiting your business may also be used to arrange your personal affairs so that ownership ends up with those family members to whom you had intended to convey ownership.
- You may wish to make changes to the management or Board of Directors of your company upon your death.

You should review your estate planning and your will every time there is a major change in your personal circumstances or relevant laws. An annual review would be prudent. Laws relating to inheritance and taxation are very specific to each jurisdiction; you should seek expert advice from an experienced party. While the subject is not usually difficult, it does require concerted thought, followed by action. Going through the exercise of estate planning and preparing your will should give you the peace of mind that you have looked after your family and loved ones to the best of your ability.

## USE OF INSURANCE IN YOUR EXIT STRATEGY

Insurance can be an interesting tool in Business Exit Planning. How you use insurance really depends on your objectives. I will provide a brief overview of some of the possible use of insurance both prior to or after a Transaction.

Prior to a Transaction, your business may be at risk in the case of your disability or death. (As Stephen Leacok, a Canadian writer, once said: "I detest life insurance agents; they always argue that I shall some day die, which is not so.") While most people have certain responsibilities to those around them, business owners/managers have a particularly high degree of responsibility, as they may be responsible for safeguarding dozens or hundreds of jobs. In such cases, it may make sense to purchase life insurance or disability insurance. You could purchase insurance on behalf of your family, on behalf of the business, or both. This way, both your family and your business will have a supplemental source of revenue during the months following death or disability, to help bridge cash flow until an investor or succession plan is found.

Some businesses have even used insurance proceeds of this nature to augment compensation to senior managers (sometimes referred to as stay bonuses), to reduce their tendency to jump ship in a time of crisis. Another type of pre-Transaction insurance that you might consider is insurance to cover estate tax. Estate taxes often catch successors by surprise, and there is often insufficient liquidity to pay them.

As for post-Transaction insurance, if you have sold less than 100 percent of your business or have agreed to an **Earn-Out**, one of the most interesting strategies available is to use insurance to fund a **Buy-Sell Agreement** among shareholders. Having a co-investor in a business can be an excellent way of ensuring that the business survives the shareholders, and this can be further facilitated with a Buy-Sell Agreement among the shareholders, whereby the death or incapacity of one shareholder imposes an obligation on the other shareholder(s) to buy, using insurance proceeds.

> The devil is in the detail!

A couple of general comments: this information is subject to a cost/benefit analysis; and you would be well advised to find an insurance professional capable of guiding you through these considerations. Obviously, it's crucial to check the fine print of any insurance documentation. One of the big loopholes in any insurance policy that you need to look for is that of pre-existing conditions. In other words, if you have a particular condition (e.g., a heart condition) at the time of writing your policy, and you die or are disabled by that condition (e.g., a heart attack), you may not receive compensation under your policy. The devil is in the detail!

# CHAPTER 8

# Finalizing Your Exit Strategy

*When I started out in business, I spent a great deal of time researching every detail that might be pertinent to the deal I was interested in making. I still do the same today. People often comment on how quickly I operate, but the reason I can move quickly is that I've done the background work first, which no one usually sees. I prepare myself thoroughly, and then when it is time to move ahead, I am ready to sprint.*

—Donald Trump (b. 1946)
American business magnate

This chapter is intended to wrap up the subject of **Business Exit Planning** as well as to serve as a bridge into the subject of **Transaction Management**. With these objectives in mind, it is organized into the following sections:

- Identifying investors, or at least classes of investors, for your company
- Should you have an asking price for your company?
- Should a competitive process be used in the sale of your company?
- Contingency plan (in case of death or incapacity prior to a **Transaction**)
- Communicating with other shareholders
- Business Exit Planning report

The first three issues should be considered even at the Business Exit Planning stage, even though they are related to the execution of a Transaction.

The tabling of a comprehensive Business Exit Planning report provides the thorough preparation which allows one to move all the more rapidly when one moves on to execute the Transaction. This will help reduce the time your company is on the market, and enhance the chances of success.

## WHAT TYPE OF INVESTORS SHOULD BE TARGETED?

There are different types of investors you might look for when selling your business:

■ *Financial investors:* Financial investors, broadly defined, include venture capital funds (for start-ups or companies early into their life cycle), angel investors (for smaller companies), and private equity funds. It is the private equity funds who are most active with mid-sized companies. As the name implies, financial investors typically bring equity finance and expertise, primarily of a financial nature, although many financial investors also pride themselves on bringing value-added knowledge in other areas, such as strategic thinking, corporate governance, restructuring, or sometimes even specialized industry sectors, such as logistics or food and beverages.

Each financial investor will have criteria for eligible investments that are clearly set, such as geographic scope, minimum and maximum investment size, or industry sectors of preference. Private equity firms seldom want to purchase companies outright; the more common focus is an investment of equity, preferred equity, or mezzanine financing to take advantage of growth opportunities, usually while continuing to work with current management, who retain an interest in the company.

Private equity firms like to do what is known as recapitalization: if your company is growing rapidly, and needs large amounts of capital, they would be very interested in purchasing the majority of your shares, plus infusing new growth capital into your firm, so that they end up with total ownership in the range of 80 to 85 percent. They would want you fully committed until they exit, and there is a potential for you to earn even more transaction revenues on the sale of your 15 to 20 percent interest, than on the original sale of your majority interest. This works well for owners who want to exit to a large extent financially, but still want to remain active with the business. The big question is: are you prepared to work for someone else?

The big question is: Are you prepared to work for someone else?

Some private equity firms may also be willing to buy companies outright—and allow more flexibility for current management to depart— where they already own a company within the industry sector in question, treating the newly purchased company as a bolt-on investment.

■ *Strategic investors:* Strategic investors have one or more industry specializations and include multinational corporations. A strategic investor may wish to diversify vertically (e.g., a steel producer may wish to acquire a steel distribution company or an iron ore mine, to have greater control over the value chain) or horizontally (e.g., a producer of peanuts may wish to acquire a producer of cashew nuts in order to offer a broader array of products to its clientele).

■ *Private individuals:* Sometimes wealthy individuals will also want to buy businesses. This is particularly true for smaller businesses.

Whether you target a financial or strategic investor depends on your objectives. For example, a strategic investor may be preferable where an owner/manager wishes to exit as soon as possible and does not wish to stay on for several years, as a financial investor would generally require, or where there may be synergies in such a strategic combination (see Box 8.1). One of our clients insisted on a financial investor because he had intellectual property to which he did not want a potential competitor (e.g., strategic investor) to have access.

Most owner/managers generally solicit interest from both strategic and financial investors, as well as wealthy individuals, as this broadens the

---

### BOX 8.1   AN IT COMPANY

An IT company offered a suite of services aimed at telecom operators, primarily creating an inventory of all equipment on the company's network, and monitoring and reporting on the status of the equipment. The company conducted the vast majority of its sales within one particular country.

The owner of the IT company felt that by becoming part of an international or regional group, there would be two strategic advantages. First, it would obtain a vehicle for marketing its products more broadly in an international or regional context. And second, there would be an opportunity to market and sell the strategic partner's IT services in the local market, thereby greatly diversifying the product line. Last but not least, the owner saw such a link-up with a strategic partner as a way of exiting gradually from his business over a three-to-seven year horizon and with an **Earn-Out**, thereby reaping some more of the upside.

market of potentially interested investors, creating healthy competitive pressures.

While the investment criteria of wealthy individuals is quite idiosyncratic, and depends on the objectives and modus operandi of the individual, Table 8.1 summarizes some of the key distinctions between financial and strategic investors.

## SHOULD THERE BE A LISTING OR ASKING PRICE?

Typically listing or asking prices are used by real estate or business brokers (e.g., in the sale of small businesses worth up to a few million euro) or by business brokers. A listing or asking price should *not* typically be used for medium- to larger-sized businesses. But why is this?

> Value, just like beauty, is in the eye of the beholder

Value, just like beauty, is in the eye of the beholder. You never know what surprisingly attractive offer you might receive, particularly in the context of a competitive bidding process. We have already discussed the possibility of synergies for investors, which are often unpredictable and may generate an offer substantially higher than a company's standalone value. Euro-Phoenix once had a business owner who believed his business was worth €15 million, and that was supported by a valuation from his accountant. Thanks to our no asking price system, we were successful in selling the business for €25 million, because interested investors bid up the price.

## SHOULD THERE BE A COMPETITIVE PROCESS?

A competitive process is like a controlled auction. There are many different types of competitive processes, some of them formal, some informal. You may have a one-, two-, three-, or more step process (e.g., a non-binding or binding bid submitted at each step).

Think of a funnel with various levels: you might approach dozens or hundreds of potential investors to test their interest with a teaser or a phone call. There might only be 10 to 15 investors who receive an **Information Memorandum (IM)** and only a handful who gain entry to the **Data Room**. Although it would be theoretically possible to negotiate a **Sale and Purchase Agreement (SPA)** simultaneously with two or more parties, typically, by the

**TABLE 8.1**   Main differences between financial and strategic investors

| | Financial Investor | Strategic Investor |
|---|---|---|
| Control | Typically allows the local owner day-to-day operational control. Some will insist on owning at least 51%, while others will agree to take a minority interest. Most financial investors will wish to take full control of management if the Business Plan is not consistently delivered. Business Plans are generally developed jointly with the owner. | Will usually require total control, as a strategic investor will typically be focused on merging into global or regional operations to gain synergies. |
| Expertise | Typically brings great financial and often strategic expertise, sometimes operating experience in specific industries, and almost certainly considerable expertise in corporate governance. | Typically brings know-how, technology, systems, access to markets and operating expertise within the sector in question. May also bring experience in finance and corporate governance. |
| Time horizon | Typically a three–five-year investment horizon. Will want to know the exit strategy prior to seriously considering an investment. | Long-term focus. Generally not concerned about exit. |
| Motivation | Very focused on financial returns over the above time frame (e.g., typically an **Internal Rate of Return (IRR)** in the range of 20–30% per annum). Will normally require a detailed business plan demonstrating returns. The business plan is generally initially developed by the owner, then fine-tuned and agreed jointly by both parties. | Not as concerned about IRR. More concerned about operational synergies with the investor's existing operations. May or may not require a business plan. |
| Management | Quality of existing management is generally vital to the transaction, as financial investors will typically try to tie in the management for at least several years with equity participation. | Quality of management is important for many strategic investors, particularly where there is a scarcity of management resources, but less so for others who have their own management that can be parachuted into the company. |

time the process has reached that stage, you would only negotiate an SPA with one party (although a strong element of competition would continue to exist if the investor realized that there was another one or more investors waiting in the wings, in the event that negotiations reached a dead end).

Where there is extremely strong interest in the company being sold, the competition is not just to see who will be the ultimate investor; there is also competition at each step in the process as to which investors proceed to the next level (e.g., which investors receive the IM or proceed to the data room).

## WHY USE A COMPETITIVE PROCESS IN SELLING A BUSINESS?

In our experience, a competitive process the high offer received for any particular company is on average two to two-and-a-half times the low offer.

A competitive process has numerous advantages for many businesses:

- *It drives up price:* An auction process generally unleashes the competitive spirit of bidders, sometimes driving prices to stratospheric levels, and the effect is no different when a competitive (e.g., controlled auction) process is applied to selling companies. From my experience in working on the sale of more than 200 companies, in a competitive process the high offer received for any particular company is on average two to two-and-a-half times the low offer. Why is this? Different investors have different levels of motivation for buying a particular company. Some investors might view the target company as a highly desirable and synergistic strategic investment. Other investors might be bottom fishers, seeking to scoop up distressed assets (see Box 8.2).
- *Better terms and conditions:* The terms and conditions of a Transaction are at least as important as the price. A competitive process typically allows the investor to negotiate much better terms and conditions. Very simply, an investor is more motivated to accept the seller's terms if there are other investors willing to step into his or her shoes.
- *A more compatible investor:* The benefits extend beyond price. Where the seller gets to know numerous investors, there are improved chances of finding a more compatible one, where there is good personal chemistry and confidence about satisfying whatever concerns or objectives a

---

### BOX 8.2    A STEEL-FRAME CONSTRUCTION COMPANY

Three non-binding offers were received for a steel-frame construction company. One was for €10 million, another was in the high 20s, and the third was in the low 30s. Ironically, the company was sold to the investor that had submitted the offer for €10 million for a total purchase price of €25 million. The bidder dramatically improved his bid when it came to the binding bid, in full realization that there were higher competitive bids at the non-binding stage. Such is the power of a competitive process.

---

### BOX 8.3    AN ENERGY COMPANY

Euro-Phoenix had completed the Data Room phase of a Transaction for a particular energy company with three investors, and had advanced to negotiating the SPA with the investor who had submitted the most attractive binding offer. Our investor suddenly withdrew due to regulatory uncertainties. No matter. Within days, the runner-up, who had already completed the Data Room, stepped into his shoes, and closed within two or three weeks. Had there not been a competitive process, it would have taken a minimum of six months to restart negotiations with another investor, go through the **Due Diligence** phase, and possibly close a Transaction.

---

seller may have (e.g., grow and improve the business, treat staff well, or observe covenants towards the seller).

■ *Higher probability of successful closing:* The more investors that compete to buy a company, the higher the likelihood that one of them will successfully complete a Transaction.

■ *It may be faster:* In a competitive process, if one bidder drops out, there is no need to restart the whole process; there is much less retracing of steps to do (see Box 8.3).

Also, from a psychological point of view, my experience is that investors move faster if they are aware that there is real competition for the target company in question.

> Investors move faster if they are aware that there is real competition for the target company in question

Virtually all private equity firms, and quite a few strategic investors, will sift through a huge number of opportunities. As one private equity professional told me, for every hundred or so deals that they look at, they will perform Due Diligence on five to eight, and perhaps close on one. Under such circumstances, you should allow for a natural process of attrition as investors fall by the wayside, for whatever reasons, during the negotiations and Due Diligence process.

## WHAT ARE THE POSSIBLE DRAWBACKS OF A COMPETITIVE PROCESS?

The drawbacks are few, and usually manageable:

- *Confidentiality:* By providing more parties with information (IM, Data Room, etc.) the chances of competitive information leaking out into the marketplace may be higher. However, there are ways of delaying the release of truly sensitive information that can help manage this risk.
- *Additional resources and more preparation:* A competitive process will generally require a greater degree of preparation and more resources. Someone will need to contact dozens or even hundreds of investors, warm them up to the process, field their questions, arrange the signing of their Confidentiality Agreements, receive and evaluate their offers, and so on. At the Data Room stage, it will be necessary to coordinate access of multiple bidders, field their numerous and penetrating questions, organize meetings with management, organize site visits, and so on.

Many business owners erroneously conclude that the high degree of preparation for a competitive process means that the process takes longer. The opposite is usually the case: up-front preparation generally allows the back end of the process to move much faster. Hence, the time during which the company is on the market will be shorter, thereby minimizing the potential for losing clients or staff due to the company being for sale.

A competitive process is almost always the preferred way for you to attract an investor. If you have negotiated and closed a deal with a single investor (e.g., using a non-competitive process), without having systematically canvassed the market, how will you know you have concluded the best possible deal, with respect not just to price, but also to satisfying all of your objectives?

> The decision to exit your business is driven by three factors: timing, timing, timing.

## TIMING YOUR EXIT

Real estate professionals talk of real estate decisions being driven by three factors: location, location, location. Likewise, the decision to exit your business is driven by three factors: timing, timing, timing.

The three aspects of the timing of a sale process (in no particular order) are:

1. *Market conditions:* In every 10-year cycle, there are usually two or three excellent years to exit, when equity market prices are high and exit conditions are excellent, as well as two or three mediocre years, when valuations are fair, but not excellent. And there may be four or five years where valuations for most (but not all!) businesses are poor, when exit is either not possible or would carry low valuations for most businesses. Obviously, exit is easier, faster, and generally occurs at the highest valuations during the really buoyant equity markets.

2. *The life cycle of your business:* How much time is required to achieve your strategy and Business Plan? Every business has a natural growth cycle: inception, growth, and maturity. Some businesses reach maturity, and then a new idea or market opening provides the opportunity for another growth spurt. Every business makes investments, and it may take years for those investments to bear fruit. The best valuation is often achieved as a company is approaching maturity (but not yet fully mature!): when not too much in the way of additional investments is required, and past investments are yielding secure and still-growing cash flows.

3. *Your own personal objectives:* What are your own personal objectives and cycle with regard to the business? Are you passionate about the business or bored? Are you willing to put in the effort and hours required to own and manage your business? Will your health permit this, and if so, for how much longer?

Part of the reason that owners sometimes procrastinate is that they are consciously or subconsciously waiting for all three aspects to be in alignment. Like an eclipse of the sun, however, these alignments seldom occur. You might be waiting a very long time indeed.

One strategy is to have your company in a state of readiness to commence a sale process. In this way, you may commence an **Initial Public Offering (IPO)** or start a competitive sales process with strategic and financial investors when market conditions are favorable.

## COMMUNICATING WITH OTHER SHAREHOLDERS

If you have co-shareholders, the Business Exit Planning process may be complicated by the need to accommodate additional stakeholders. Depending on whether you are a majority or minority shareholder in a public or private corporation, you may have obligations to seek consent from other shareholders.

Consensual approaches are typically more fruitful (and pleasant) than conflictual. If you have only one or just a handful of co-shareholders or minority shareholders, the objective should be to agree on a course of action that is acceptable to all. In many situations, for example, co-shareholders or minority shareholders are willing, and often even eager, to exit at the same time as the majority shareholder. In such cases, it is usually preferable that any mandate for legal, accounting, tax, financial, and other advisors be given by all shareholders, rather than just by the controlling shareholder, with expenses shared pro rata according to shareholdings.

Where a minority shareholder does not want to exit, that may introduce an additional level of complexity. Does the minority shareholder perhaps want to purchase your shares? If so, would he or she be prepared to offer a reasonable valuation? Or would the minority shareholder sell to you at a favorable valuation? Are there first rights of refusal or **Put/Call Options** among the different shareholders? A legal advisor and perhaps a financial advisor should be consulted to advise you in such situations.

A company with numerous shareholders may be a deterrent for some investors who don't want the headache of managing relations with so many shareholders, particularly if they are not in alignment or not speaking with one voice. Where the company is a publically listed company, a purchaser may also face the possibility of class action suits from minority shareholders. Once again, consult your advisors. A possible strategy might be for one or more of the larger shareholders to buy out the small shareholders. Often this can be done on quite favorable terms.

If you are mandating a corporate finance advisor with respect to a Business Exit Planning mandate, you may want to include a review of the minority shareholders situation, and a strategy for dealing with this issue in the scope of services.

## YOUR CONTINGENCY PLAN

A Business Exit Planning exercise cannot be considered complete unless there has been contingency planning for the possible death or disability of the owner/manager, perhaps even the senior members of the management team. The problem may be particularly important to address if the business owner and the CEO are the same person. If death or disability were to occur, what changes in governance would you want at your company?

- Would there be any changes to the Board of Directors, CEO, or other senior management functions?
- Would there be any change to signing authorities?
- What directions would you give to your estate? If the business were to be sold, who would you want to run such a process? What guidance would you want to give them (in terms of price, possibly interested investors, etc.)?

> The lack of a contingency plan and will has created many major family feuds which may have been avoided with appropriate planning.

The contingency plan should be documented and signed by you, the owner, along with the necessary witnesses, with a copy retained with the appropriate legal advisor. The lack of a contingency plan and will has created many major family feuds which may have been avoided with appropriate planning.

## BUSINESS EXIT PLANNING REPORT

As Napoleon Hill once wrote, "Reduce your plan to writing. The moment you complete this, you will have definitely given form to the intangible desire." The same holds true for your Exit Plan.

If you are working with a financial advisor, it may be worth instructing the advisor to create a Business Exit Planning report at the conclusion of this phase of initial analysis or Business Exit Planning, that would summarize all or a portion of the following subjects:

- Summary of shareholders' objectives. What are your own motivations for seeking a **Business Exit?**
- Summary of the company's objectives (as these objectives may differ from those of the shareholders). How much is your business worth (assuming the appropriate valuation methodologies have been appropriately applied)? Does this meet with your expectations and satisfy your personal goals?
- Valuation (according to appropriate valuation methodologies).
- What are potential obstacles to a Transaction (skeletons in the closet) or what are possible value enhancements to the business that you may wish to take on before transferring ownership?
- What options for Business Exit strategy might be considered (**Management Buyout [MBO]**, merger, minority or majority sale, etc.) that satisfy your objectives? The advisors' views as to the pros and cons of each option, along with the likelihood of success, should also be provided.
- What are the current market conditions for exit?
- Marketing strategy (types of investors that are likely to be interested). How saleable is your business? Is the profile of your business likely to be a strategic fit for investors (e.g., not too fragmented, or in unrelated lines of business). What processes might be considered for exit?
- What are the ways in which value might be enhanced prior to exit? How might one achieve these?
- Tax planning.
- Estate planning.
- Accommodation of co-shareholders or minority shareholders.
- Contingency plan.
- The types of processes that best satisfy the shareholders' and company's objectives, and a suggested timeline that satisfies these objectives.

Notice that the previous headings cover just about everything we have covered in Part I of this book, on the subject of Business Exit Planning.

Once your advisor provides this Business Exit Planning report, if it is not acted upon immediately in terms of moving to a Transaction, it would be worthwhile to revisit and update it on an annual basis.

# Two

# Managing the Transaction

*Deals are my art form. Other people paint beautifully on canvas or write wonderful poetry. I like making deals, preferably big deals. That's how I get my kicks.*

—Donald Trump (b. 1946)
American business magnate

In Part I, I described the process of planning a **Business Exit**. In Part II, I will deal with some of the principles you, as a business owner, should keep in mind when managing a **Transaction**.

I have organized Part II into the following three chapters:

■ Chapter 9: The Transaction process: Because the sale of all or a portion of the ownership interest in a company is the most common form of exit, I will approach **Transaction Management** from this perspective. I'm not saying that selling your business is the only exit option. But even though there are numerous and genuine options for a business exit, selling is the most common one for mid-sized businesses. Furthermore, even if you are doing a **Management Buyout** (MBO) or an **Intergenerational Transfer**, there are elements from this chapter that may still apply.

The competitive sale process as I've defined in this book is the one most often used by my firm, Euro-Phoenix. We find this to be generally applicable for the sale of mid-sized companies, and have refined it into a tried and tested process. There may be circumstances, however, where other types of processes, or no process at all, simply a negotiated sale, are more appropriate. I add a small addendum for selling a company in a non-competitive process.

- Chapter 10: Negotiating a Transaction: Negotiation is part art, part science. This section is not designed to teach business owners to negotiate your own Transactions, merely to make you sensitive to some of the most important issues that are relevant for selecting and supervising your advisors.
- Chapter 11: Cross-border Transactions: Transactions for larger and mid-sized companies are increasingly cross-border. The world seems to be shrinking. This opens up new opportunities as well as challenges for business owners.

# CHAPTER 9

# The Transaction Process

*People get caught up in wonderful, eye-catching pitches, but they don't do enough to close the deal. It's no good if you don't make the sale. Even if your foot is in the door or you bring someone into a conference room, you don't win the deal unless you actually get them to sign on the dotted line.*

—Donald Trump (b. 1946)
American business magnate

This chapter is intended to give business owners a bird's eye view of an entire **Transaction** process. While the Transaction chosen here is a typical sell side process, there would also be great similarities in how other Transactions are managed, such as a capital injection from private equity firms. The main sections in this chapter are:

- Overview of a competitive process
- Confidentiality through a Transaction process
- Involving company staff in the Transaction process and communicating with investors
- Marketing your opportunity: From Long List to Short List
- The **Information Memorandum (IM)**
- Nonbinding offers
- **Due Diligence**
- Binding offers
- Exclusivity
- Transaction structuring
- **Heads of Agreement**
- **Sale and Purchase Agreement (SPA)**
- Closing the Transaction
- Noncompetitive processes

As the above headings suggest, this chapter is perhaps the meatiest and most action-packed in the book. I recommend that a company finalize as much of the preparation as possible (e.g., preparing the IM and the **Data Room**) before going public by approaching investors, once again to avoid slippage in the process once investors have been approached.

## OVERVIEW OF A COMPETITIVE PROCESS

I am a huge believer in competition in just about every context, not just selling companies. With respect to selling companies, I've seen numerous cases where a competitive process has produced results far beyond the sellers' expectations. There is something about a competitive process that stimulates investors, in the same way as at an art auction, where prices may be bid up to stratospheric levels. Sometimes stratospheric prices may be rational (e.g., where there may be significant synergies), and sometimes they may be due to irrational exuberance (don't underestimate the role of ego in the psyches of alpha males typically in charge of acquisitions).

> Don't underestimate the role of ego in the psyches of alpha males typically in charge of acquisitions.

There are varying degrees of competitive processes, from a very formal, multi-stage process, to a very informal process, with few or no rules, that might not even be called a process, but is still competitive: the seller is entertaining negotiations with multiple investors simultaneously. In a competitive process, none of the bidders should know the identity of the other bidders. This reduces the potential of collusion among the investors.

Your corporate finance advisor will be best equipped to advise you on what form of process is most appropriate for your situation. It is inappropriate to prescribe any kind of process until the seller or the seller's advisor has talked to potential bidders, because a process should be designed according to the number of bidders likely to participate, their requirements, desires, informational requirements, timelines, and so on (See Table 9.1).

> There are elements of the timeline that fall completely outside of the ambit of the financial advisor.

**TABLE 9.1**   Overview of the Sale of a Company by Competitive Process

| PHASE I | INFORMATION PREPARATION | MARKETING |
|---|---|---|
| 4–8 WEEKS | ▪ Teaser (FA)*<br>▪ Information Memorandum (FA)*<br>▪ Data Room (FA)*<br>▪ Confidentiality Agreement (FA)(L) | ▪ Assemble Long List (FA)<br>▪ Calls (FA)<br>▪ Short List (FA) |

| PHASE II | SOLICIT NON-BINDING BIDS |
|---|---|
| 4–6 WEEKS | ▪ Investors sign Confidentiality Agreement (I)<br>▪ Investors receive Information Memorandum and Process Letter (I)<br>▪ Investors submit nonbinding Offer with Valuation (I)<br>▪ Evaluation of bids by Vendor (V with assistance of FA) |

| PHASE III | DUE DILIGENCE |
|---|---|
| 4–8 WEEKS | ▪ Data Room (FA)*<br>▪ Site Visits (S, FA)<br>▪ Management Presentations (S, FA)<br>▪ Questions and Answers (S, all advisors)<br>▪ Submission of Binding Bids (I) |

| PHASE IV | LEGAL AGREEMENTS |
|---|---|
| 1–4 WEEKS | ▪ Sale and Purchase Agreement (L, input from S and all advisors)<br>▪ Shareholders' Agreement (L, input from S, possibly other advisors)<br>▪ Employment Agreements (L, input from S)<br>▪ Other agreements |

| PHASE V | SATISFY CONDITIONS AND CLOSING |
|---|---|
| 1–10 WEEKS | ▪ Obtain new financing, if necessary (I)<br>▪ Obtain approval of banks for transfer of debt, where necessary (S)<br>▪ Obtain Competition Office approvals, if required (S,L)<br>▪ Satisfy other conditions, as per SPA (S, L)<br>▪ Obtain Board approvals of investors and/or sellers (S)<br>▪ Closing (S, I, L, FA) |

S: Seller; L: Legal advisor; I: Investor; FA: Financial Advisor
*based on information prepared by seller

All indications as to timing are purely indicative. Figure 9.1 indicates that it may be theoretically possible to close a transaction within 10 weeks. Table 9.1 provides further detail. As a financial advisor, I am often pressured to commit to timelines. My standard answer is that I may commit to things that are under our control, but there are elements of the timeline that fall completely outside of the ambit of the financial advisor:

- Information provision by the seller, with respect to the information necessary for the **Teaser**, IM, and Data Room. In my experience, 10 weeks might be typical for information provision, and that's only one step in the process.
- Timing of the investors. Financial advisors cannot, at the commencement of a sale process, accurately predict how long investors will take to make their decisions, obtain board approvals, and so on.

We have seen processes progress rapidly from inception to closure within four or five months; we have also seen others (see Box 6.1) take more than two years. The average, you might say, is about nine months. It's like giving birth.

## CONFIDENTIALITY THROUGH A TRANSACTION PROCESS

Confidentiality with respect to exit is probably one of your primary concerns as a business owner. Even an unconfirmed rumor about your company being for sale could cause damage. The type of information disclosure necessary to consummate a Transaction may put a company at a serious competitive disadvantage if that information ends up in the wrong hands (see Box 9.1).

> If you cannot trust your own senior management, that puts you in a very difficult situation.

Protection of a company that is pursuing a Transaction essentially stems from several sources: (a) a confidentiality or NonDisclosure Agreement; (b) a deliberate strategy to delay transmission of sensitive information to bidders to the last point in the process where it may be legitimately transmitted without causing undue stress to the investors; (c) dealing only with reputable investors whose reputations would be placed at risk in the event of a breach of confidentiality; and (d) not dealing with direct competitors

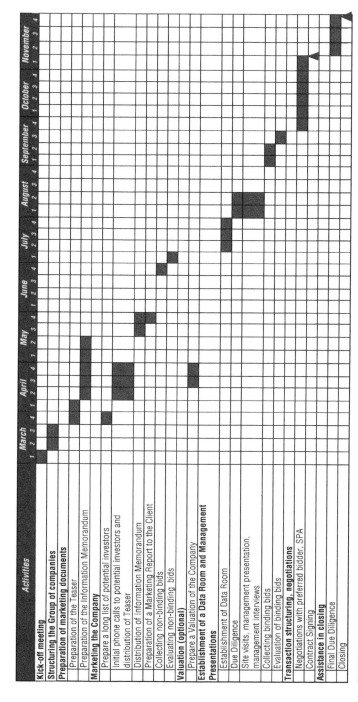

**FIGURE 9.1** Indicative GANTT
Source: Euro-Phoenix

## BOX 9.1    A MEAT BUSINESS

A private equity firm retained Euro-Phoenix to sell a company in the meat business. The client insisted that the key managers of the company be apprised of the sale; indeed, their cooperation was necessary to furnish us with the information for the IM. Six weeks into the assignment, I received an urgent call from our client. I rushed over to its offices, only to learn that the five key managers of the firm had left to set up their own competing firm, and had taken many of the company's clients with them. Our mandate was called off, as the company was obviously unsellable in such a situation. The company never recovered.

While this is a very rare and extreme case, it does illustrate what can happen if the wrong people learn about your business being for sale, or if you trust the wrong people with sensitive information. But if you cannot trust your own senior management, that puts you in a very difficult situation.

or even indirect competitors, or if dealing with them, perhaps further tightening the conditions.

Most owners have a healthy skepticism regarding the ability of Confidentiality Agreements alone to adequately protect the confidentiality of their information, given the difficulty of proving a breach in the first place and then the amount of damages. Hence the need to rely on a combination of all four approaches.

### Confidentiality Agreements

Confidentiality agreements (also known as nondisclosure agreements) are typically drafted and negotiated by the seller's legal or financial advisor. Generally speaking, boilerplate agreements do a poor job of properly representing the interests of the parties concerned; this is an agreement that requires careful thought and specific focus. Confidentiality Agreements will stipulate that confidential information received by the investor will remain confidential, at least for a stipulated time (typically two to three years). In some situations (e.g., where the investor provides financial information), the investor may also require the seller to sign a Confidentiality Agreement, or one agreement may be negotiated that mutually binds both parties to confidentiality.

Some investors are quite adamant that their entering into negotiations with a particular company should also be treated as confidential. Investors that are publicly listed on a stock exchange are particularly sensitive in this respect, as the stock exchange typically prescribes strict disclosure rules with respect to negotiating Transactions.

A Confidentiality Agreement should state that the fact that discussions are taking place or materials have been exchanged is also to remain confidential. A key section of the Confidentiality Agreement is defining the scope of information or material that is confidential: sellers will generally try to broaden the scope, while investors will try to narrow it. The Confidentiality Agreement will typically stipulate that the information defined as confidential may be used solely for the purpose of evaluating a Transaction. It may limit the number of individuals within the investor's organization who have access to confidential information. The investor either takes responsibility for confidentiality with respect to information distributed to its advisors, or the advisors should each sign a separate Confidentiality Agreement.

Because an investor will come in contact with your company's staff during a Due Diligence process, it may also be beneficial to include a non-solicitation clause in the Confidentiality Agreement—namely, that the investor will neither induce any of your staff to leave your company to join its company, nor enter into any discussions in this regard.

Sellers sometimes try to stipulate liquidated damages (e.g., predefined damages if a breach of confidentiality is proven), as well as what material should be returned or destroyed in the event that negotiations break off. These can be particularly sticky points. The negotiation of Confidentiality Agreements can sometimes be quite difficult. There are also issues pertaining to the choice of law (whether disputes will be resolved by arbitration or litigation) and who will bear the costs. The Confidentiality Agreement is typically the first legal agreement negotiated between an investor and a seller; its importance is often overlooked.

## Transmission of Information to Investors

> The volume and degree of confidential information transmitted by a company should be in proportion to the degree of commitment given by an investor.

There is a general principle that should be observed in these Transactions: The volume and degree of confidential information transmitted by a company should be in proportion to the degree of commitment given by an investor. For example, in the first stage of information disclosure (typically a **Teaser**), when there is no commitment from the investor, usually there is not sufficient information to ascertain the identity of the company (although there should be enough information to allow the investor to decide whether or not to proceed, e.g., sign a Confidentiality Agreement).

Once a Confidentiality Agreement is signed, the company usually provides investors with an IM. IMs typically divulge a considerable amount of information about the company, including its identity, key market and financial data, staffing, backlog of contracts, and so on. In cases where certain information may be extremely sensitive (e.g., the identity of clients), the names or identities of clients are sometimes withheld and instead the IM might refer to Client 1, Client 2, and so on, with an understanding that the identities of clients or other sensitive information would be revealed at some later stage before closing.

After the IM is received, investors generally proceed to the next level of commitment, which is to provide a nonbinding offer. Once the parties agree to the terms of an offer (often finalized in a **Term Sheet**), the company then allows access to the Data Room, where source documents such as contracts, title documents, intellectual property, and so on, are made available. Once again, highly sensitive information may be withheld until prior to closing, bearing in mind that if such information is not according to the investor's expectations, the investor will generally reserve the right to back out of the Transaction. Withholding sensitive information, however, has the effect of hindering the seller's ability to nail down the purchase price in an unconditional way. Typically, the withholding of information results in any discussion on pricing being conditional on there being no surprises in the withheld information.

After the Data Room, the investor then must decide whether to make a binding offer. After a binding offer, the parties usually negotiate an SPA. Before signing the SPA, the investor will generally insist on receiving all the information about the company, with absolutely nothing withheld. A former client of Euro-Phoenix stated when selling its business: "We had to undress to our underwear, and beyond." Indeed, undressing is the quid pro quo for the investor risking his or her millions.

## Dealing with a Reputable Party

A Confidentiality Agreement, or indeed any other agreement, is usually not worth the paper it is written on unless it is signed by a reputable party. Given the difficulty of verification of any transgressions and proof of damages, a judgment needs to be made about the character of the individual or corporate recipient; there must be mutual trust in order for a deal to work. This is, of course, especially true when providing sensitive information to a direct competitor and so the ethics and reputation of the firm in question are vitally important. Some parties, for example, have a reputation for litigation. This applies not only to signing a confidentiality agreement with an investor, but in general, to bringing an investor into the process as well.

### Not Dealing with Direct or Indirect Competitors

Most business owners have a healthy reluctance to share information with competitors. The more direct the potential competitive threat, the stronger the reluctance. If a business owner has other potential investors, he or she might choose to negotiate first with parties who do not pose a threat. Alternatively, once again, the release of sensitive information could be delayed. In doing so there is a tradeoff, however, in that this may also delay obtaining a bona fide offer.

> Think of the process of information disclosure as a ritual or dance: step by step. Do not let one foot (information provided to the investor) get too far ahead of the other (commitment by the investor)!

Think of the process of information disclosure as a ritual or dance: step by step. Do not let one foot (information provided to the investor) get too far ahead of the other (commitment by the investor)!

## INVOLVING COMPANY STAFF IN THE TRANSACTION PROCESS AND COMMUNICATIONS WITH INVESTORS

It is ultimately at your discretion to decide how many members of the management team to involve in the sale process, as well as the extent and timing of that involvement. Of paramount importance, of course, is confidentiality: the wider the circle, the greater the likelihood of a breach of confidentiality. News has a habit of spreading within the company, and then it's only a matter of time before it spreads to outside the company. On the other hand, if you try to do too much yourself, in terms of managing or preparing data disclosure, you could easily become the bottleneck in the process.

Most owners typically hold an internal meeting of their three to five most trusted lieutenants, being perfectly candid as to what is happening and explaining the need for confidentiality. This meeting is usually held at the beginning of the IM preparation phase, when the heavy lifting generally begins.

If you want to delegate the responsibility of spearheading the internal management team engaged in **Business Exit Planning** and **Transaction Management**, and if your firm has a strong CFO, he or she might make an excellent candidate to lead the internal core team. Much of the information required for the Teaser, IM, Data Room, and **Management Presentation** is financial in nature. And, of course, the entire valuation process is driven by financial information. Your CFO will play an important role within the management team in initially liaising with financial advisors and preparing information for investors; as a Transaction progresses, there will be need for even more detailed financial disclosure to investors. Other members of your internal team might be your head of production (if you are a production company), your head of sales and marketing, and your internal legal advisor. Of course much depends on the competencies of the individuals and their ability to maintain confidentiality.

As owner or CEO, you should also clearly delineate who is responsible for delivering what deliverables for the IM, and under what deadlines. This will represent a large workload for this group of people during a three-to-eight-week period, and you will need to ensure the proper prioritization among competing tasks. The running of a sale process generally takes a substantial amount of time from the daily running of the business, even if advisors are doing most of the work. It is essential that you balance and communicate priorities so that the core team will have the necessary time available for the Business Exit Planning and Transaction Management. You, yourself, will also need to make time available: for numerous consultations with stakeholders, selecting and supervising advisors, giving direction to your internal core team, and attending myriad meetings and negotiations with investors.

> Where a company retains a financial advisor, all communications to and from investors should be channeled through him or her.

The issue of communications with investors is also an important one. Where a company retains a financial advisor, all communications to and from investors should be channeled through him or her, or at least coordinated. There are a number of reasons for this:

- It is generally the responsibility of the financial advisor to ensure that all bidders are on a level playing field; that is, receive the same or very similar information. Where a direct channel of communication develops between one investor and, say, a member of the management team, it will be hard for the advisor to ensure the level playing field. If rumors start developing that one investor has an inside track, other investors may withdraw from the process.
- The investor may learn information that was not appropriate to communicate to the investor. For example, investors should not know how many bidders are in the process, nor anything about the identity of those bidders, let alone the terms and conditions of the bid. Sometimes members of the management team who are not versed in the niceties of mergers and acquisitions (M&A) will inadvertently let some information slip.
- All information related to Due Diligence that passes from the company to investors should be vetted by the financial advisor. There is a chance that this vetting process may be short-circuited, where there are communications between company staff and investors.

These considerations should hold true throughout the sale process, right through to the closing of the Transaction.

## MARKETING YOUR OPPORTUNITY: FROM LONG LIST TO SHORT LIST

Based on the principles in the marketing strategy, a list of potential investors must be assembled (the Long List). The Long List may consist of dozens or even hundreds of investors, and is assembled from the following sources:

- Investors known by the company and its advisors
- Industry contacts (associations and people who have worked many years in the industry)
- Research from databases and other public sources
- Other intermediaries

In a competitive process, it is important to have systematic and extensive coverage of the eligible investors for a particular company. In the normal course of operations, a financial advisor would check the list with you to ensure that no parties are to be excluded, for whatever reason; then begins the painstaking work of contacting all investors. At this point, everything proceeds on an anonymous basis; that is, in phone calls, investors will receive a blind description of the company (e.g., industry or sector, revenues, number of staff members, etc., but insufficient information to identify the company, and certainly not the company name). A financial advisor can contact investors on an anonymous basis. If a company representative calls an investor, your cover is blown.

Those investors who express an interest will usually immediately ask for something in writing. This is the purpose fulfilled by the Teaser. Once again, the Teaser is blind; its purpose, generally, is to provide an investor with sufficient information, that he or she may also circulate internally, to ascertain whether they wish to proceed to the next level; that is, sign a Confidentiality Agreement and receive an IM.

## THE INFORMATION MEMORANDUM

Preparation of the IM generally proceeds simultaneously with the marketing phase. In this fashion, just as the IM is completed, it may be handed over to investors, upon signature of the Confidentiality Agreement.

### What Is an IM?

An IM is a document provided by a company to prospective investors after the investors have reviewed a Teaser and signed a Confidentiality Agreement (see Table 9.2). Some business owners and financial advisors look at an IM as a marketing document that provides a selective overview of the attractive features of a company. But the IM may also be a source of risk: In some

**TABLE 9.2** Table of contents, sample IM, ABC Corporation

| | |
|---|---|
| 1 | Executive summary |
| 2 | Strategy of the company |
| 3 | Revenue segmentation and clientele |
| 4 | Financial information |
| 5 | Production |
| 6 | Human resources |
| 7 | Quality control, systems, and IT |
| 8 | Litigation |
| Appendix A: | History of the company |
| Appendix B: | The market and competitors |
| Appendix C: | List of assets |
| Appendix D: | CVs of key staff |

countries, mostly Anglo-Saxon jurisdictions, an IM by law must contain a full, true, and complete disclosure of all information that may materially affect the value of a company. Other jurisdictions may not be as strict.

A company and its financial advisor must strike a balance when preparing an IM. The document should be a marketing document, in the sense that it should motivate investors to want to invest in the company, but it should be devoid of hype, exaggeration, or omission, and should provide a complete disclosure of material facts. Hype or exaggeration will only diminish your company's credibility and its management in the eyes of investors, and may also create legal liability for those preparing the IM.

## Why Prepare an IM?

> An IM allows you to present a comprehensive, accurate, and attractive picture of your company.

In general, an IM allows you to present a comprehensive, accurate, and attractive picture of your company. The alternative is simply to respond to investors' questions, but this typically does not allow you to provide a comprehensive overview, and makes it difficult to present the information in the best light while preserving balance and accuracy. It also helps to ensure that all investors receive the same information. This is particularly crucial when a seller is running a competitive process.

The more information that finds its way into the IM, the less need there is for investors to pose written questions, saving time for both buyer and seller. Hence it enhances the efficiency of the process.

From an investor's point of view, a good IM demonstrates the professionalism and motivation to sell of the sellers, as well as the quality of the management—important factors when deciding whether to bid for a company. It, or at least extracts of it, will typically be circulated within the corporate entity of the investor. Recipients will usually include members of investment committees or boards, as well as the senior officers of the company. It's therefore important to get it right.

## How Should You Go About Preparing an IM?

Preparing an IM requires a high level of internal organization. As the business owner/manager, you should lead a small team of experts in the main areas (e.g., sales/marketing, legal, and finance) that will need to be covered.

Deliverables and deadlines should be decided for each member of the team. When this process is complete, you should review the final version along with all members of the team, to ensure its consistency, completeness, and accuracy.

When Euro-Phoenix prepares an IM, we aim to provide investors with details of clients, market position, operations, finance, risks, and so on; in other words, information sufficient for them to prepare a nonbinding bid, with an indication of the bidder's valuation of the company. An IM typically comprises 30 to 70 pages (Table 9.2). One effective way of designing the contents is to ask yourself what information you would need were you buying the company.

Given that the IM is designed to solicit a nonbinding offer for the company, with a valuation, the omission of one or more key facts may give a distorted valuation and provide an investor with an opportunity to renegotiate its offer.

### How Is the IM Likely to Be Used by Investors?

> We never get a second chance to make a first impression.

It is the most efficient way of providing a large volume of information about a company to investors. Even though there may be one person or a small group of people performing a Due Diligence check on the company at its premises, there is also a need to communicate with a wider range of decision-makers (e.g., investment committees or boards) who may never appear on-site. The IM is by far the best way to do this. A high-quality IM is critical when selling a company: in the same way that a CV may go through many drafts in order to present the candidate in the best possible light, investing time to produce a quality IM will also pay off. We never get a second chance to make a first impression.

The IM is typically distributed with what is known as a **Process Letter:** a letter that sets out the deadline for submitting offers, the form and substance of the offer (e.g., should it be an all-cash offer?), and possibly additional information such as:

- Disclosure of the decision-making structure within the investor's organization and approvals required to make the acquisition.
- Sources of financing (e.g., the Transaction may take substantially longer if the investor must seek outside financing). You may also ask investors to submit copies of their financial statements.

■ Criteria by which offers will be evaluated. Is it based on price alone? Or might there be other criteria?

## NONBINDING OFFERS

As a rule of thumb, investors are given four to six weeks to review the IM and to prepare a nonbinding offer based on the information supplied. While there is no theoretical limit to the number of bidders you allow into the Data Room, you should try to strike a balance between creating some healthy competition (i.e., having at least three participants), and not wanting to share confidential information with parties that have a very low probability of winning. If there are likely to be more companies bidding than are allowed into the Data Room, considerable competitive pressures may develop at the nonbinding-offer stage, as investors jockey to be accepted into the Due Diligence phase of the process. Once the offers start coming in, you'll need to work with your advisors to evaluate them.

If appropriate, run a credit check or financial review on the potential investors, to check the depth of their financial resources, their payment history, and so on. From this point on, each investor is likely to consume a considerable amount of company management and advisors' time—both of which cost money. In sales jargon, you must qualify the lead, or make sure that it is capable of following through with the Transaction, and isn't just on a fishing expedition to obtain information. The credit check or financial review could also be performed prior to distribution of the IM. It may also be necessary to contact one or more of the investors in order to clarify certain parts of their offer.

A financial advisor will usually provide the company with a report analyzing and assessing the strengths and weaknesses of the bids, and making a recommendation as to which investors should be permitted to proceed to the Due Diligence phase.

## DUE DILIGENCE

> The purpose of the Due Diligence phase is to provide the investors with the information they require in order to submit a binding bid.

Whereas the purpose of the IM is to provide investors with sufficient information to make a *nonbinding* bid, the purpose of the Due Diligence phase is to provide the investors with the information they require in order to submit a *binding* bid. Whereas the information in the IM was provided in summary format, the Due Diligence phase typically requires original source documents (contracts, title documents, permits, etc.).

Due Diligence allows an investor to comprehensively assess the costs, benefits, and risks of investing in a particular company. Whereas a Letter of Intent or **Term Sheet** proceeds on the assumption that all information from the seller has been correct, the Due Diligence process also allows an investor to test the quality of disclosure. Hence Due Diligence will provide the investor with the data to make two crucial decisions: Should they proceed with an investment in the company? And if so, at what valuation?

During the Due Diligence process, an investor may find one or more deal-breakers, which may give cause to back away from a Transaction (see Box 9.2). This is all the more reason to try to identify possible deal-breakers and remedy them, if possible, prior to the commencement of any sale process.

Sometimes investors don't use advisors when evaluating an IM and making a nonbinding offer, but it is very rare indeed for investors not to use advisors during the Due Diligence process and at the binding offer stage. Usually this entails an army of advisors: legal, audit, tax, financial, and sometimes environmental or other technical experts. This is not surprising: the stakes are much higher on a binding bid than on a nonbinding bid.

---

### BOX 9.2  DUE DILIGENCE OF A MINING COMPANY

On my first Due Diligence assignment as a junior investment banker, I was sent to Northern Quebec (Canada) to review the operations of a well-known Canadian copper and gold mining concern. The operations were truly impressive. I spent three days talking to management and visiting the mines (going more than 10,000 feet underground).

There was only one issue that raised a concern: almost 50 percent of the value of the assets of the company on the balance sheet was in asbestos ores. This was back in the mid-1980s, when litigation surrounding asbestos was already becoming commonplace.

This one issue constituted a deal-breaker. As there was little if any chance that the asbestos would ever be mined, this amount would likely require a write-off.

The Due Diligence process consists of several elements:

- The Data Room, with questions and answers (Q&A) on material in the Data Room
- The Management Presentation
- Site visits

> Investors' expectations are typically very high. They expect answers to all of their questions within hours or days. Otherwise their expensive advisors are spinning wheels and racking up the charges.

Due Diligence is generally by far the most intensive part of the sale process, taking place usually within a six-to-eight-week period and with as many investors as you allow to participate in the Due Diligence process during that six-to-eight-week period. It is important that no one person become a bottleneck in the process, but that the sellers establish a multidisciplinary team covering each major area (sales and marketing, legal, production, finance, taxation, and so on); possibly the same team that helped prepare the IM. Investors' expectations are typically very high. They expect answers to all of their questions within hours or days. Otherwise their expensive advisors are spinning wheels and racking up the charges.

The Due Diligence process puts considerable stress on the owner, the management team, and advisors. Thorough advance preparation will help to at least partially alleviate the stress.

An invitation to investors to participate in the Due Diligence process is typically issued in writing, once again in the form of a Process Letter. This is very similar to the one described earlier, except that it may include a few additional points:

- You might want to describe the structure of the deal:
  - Percentage of shares to be sold (or range)
  - Is real estate included or excluded, and so on
- Data Room rules should also be included (which typically cover opening hours, the number of staff members that can attend at any one time, and the dates on which the Data Room will be available). The rules ensure that the Data Room is not a free for all, but a structured process whereby each investor has access to identical information during an exclusive period.

## The Data Room

Depending on the size and complexity of the company being sold, a Data Room may contain thousands or even hundreds of thousands of documents, including all relevant client, supplier, employee, financing, and other contracts, as well as title documents, board minutes, and so on. Indeed, any document that could have an impact on the value of the company should be in the Data Room.

As the establishment of a Data Room requires an enormous amount of work on the part of seller and advisors, and often involves the disclosure of highly confidential information, most sellers insist that, as a prerequisite to providing access to a Data Room, investors should have made a nonbinding offer, and perhaps even signed a Term Sheet, that is acceptable to the sellers. The Data Room provides the detailed evidence that then permits the investor(s) to provide a binding offer within days or weeks of the closure of the Data Room.

A Data Room may be in physical form (e.g., literally a room full of data) or the seller and its advisors may opt for a virtual Data Room, which means that investors may access documents via the Internet. Sometimes the parties opt for a combination of virtual and physical Data Rooms, with the most confidential documents appearing only in the physical Data Room. One advantage of many virtual Data Rooms is that it is possible to monitor who was accessing what documents at what time (e.g., to what degree each investor is taking seriously the Due Diligence process).

In a physical Data Room, the seller's representative is usually present at all times to ensure that only authorized personnel from the investors are in attendance, that no one is making unauthorized copies or scans of information, and that legitimate information requests are coordinated. A Data Room is often governed by rules set by the seller, which investors must sign or acknowledge in order to gain access.

> Care must be taken that the investors never have occasion to meet or cross paths during the Due Diligence.

Because of the cost of running a Data Room and the need to observe timelines, each investor is usually given limited access, typically measured in days. For the seller of a business, preparing and running a Data Room is probably the most intensive phase of selling a business, given that in most sale processes Management Presentations and site visits are also usually concurrent with the opening of the Data Room. The complexity of managing this process is further augmented where there are multiple investors to be coordinated. Care must be taken that the investors never have occasion to meet or cross paths during the Due Diligence; indeed, some investors also insist that their participation in the process is kept confidential.

During the Data Room process, you and your advisors must be prepared to answer questions and provide supplementary information to investors. Answers are mostly expected within one or two days, failing which investors may ask for an extension of the period during which the Data Room is open. It may be necessary to disclose additional documents beyond what was originally contained in the Data Room.

Effective administration of the Data Room is a key ingredient to success. Keep a record of all information that was received or open for review by the investors. This will help to prevent or resolve future disputes.

You must also give consideration to how much you scrutinize the information you place in the Data Room. Much depends on the degree of confidence that you, as the business owner, have in the information going into the Data Room. Many business owners pay minimum attention to this scrutiny: they prefer to deal with issues as they arise. Other business owners insist on a full **Vendor Due Diligence**; that is, they ask their advisors to go through the full Data Room as if they were an investor, to identify every possible issue, every potential skeleton in the closet. They can then have greater confidence in opening the Data Room to investors. Conducting a Vendor Due Diligence can easily cost several tens of thousands of dollars for a mid-sized company; hence you should carefully assess the cost/benefit of running one.

When negotiating the SPA, investors will often ask for **Representations and Warranties** that the Data Room was complete, and that all of the documents in the Data Room represent a true and complete reflection of the state of affairs of the company. It is therefore vital that you and your advisors ensure the completeness and accuracy of documents in the Data Room. I know of one situation, for example, where a seller (whether deliberately or inadvertently) withheld a document from a Data Room, resulting in millions of dollars of potential liability.

> Investors often use shortcomings in the Data Room to drive down prices.

The quality of a Data Room, and how the process is managed, can make or break a sale process. It can also dramatically affect valuation, as investors often use shortcomings in the Data Room to drive down prices.

In a nutshell, there are just three words of advice when it comes to a Data Room: preparation, preparation, preparation.

## The Management Presentation

A Management Presentation is often the first time that the company's management team meets the investors. This will be a very important meeting, one that warrants extensive preparation.

Typically, a Management Presentation takes the form of key members of management speaking during a PowerPoint presentation. Ideally, each member of the management team should present his or her own section (finance, marketing, production, etc.), as this will give the investors an opportunity to assess each member of the team, and develop some comfort that the company is not a one-man show. It is worth rehearsing the Management Presentation, perhaps in the form of a dress rehearsal, where the financial advisor poses the likeliest questions to management. It is helpful if the financial advisor or an expert on presentation skills coaches the management team, advising on everything from body language to the appropriateness of the message. The entire Management Presentation should not generally last more than half a day, including a chance for informal dialogue and some interactive discussion.

Don't talk about price, deal structuring, or shareholder-related issues at the Management Presentation. This should not concern the management of the company, and may be inappropriate. Also, one of the purposes of the Management Presentation should be to build relationship capital between the owner and management team on the one hand, and the investor on the other hand. It is important to establish as strong a bond of trust and mutual respect as possible between the owner and the investor, as this will serve as an important motivation for the parties to make it through the often difficult negotiation of the SPA.

## Site Visits

Don't make assumptions. Ask the investors what they want to see: plants, offices, warehouses, and so on. Care should be observed to ensure that investors do not meet each other or cross paths during the site visits. If you have three investors doing Due Diligence, you will need to organize three different site visits. I know, I know....it would be more convenient to pack them all onto one bus, but resist the temptation! Site visits should generally be accompanied by a management representative, as well as the financial advisor. The appropriate staff (plant manager, etc.) should conduct various parts of the tour.

## BINDING OFFERS

The offers received after Due Diligence are usually binding, but subject to a number of terms and conditions:

- No material adverse change in the affairs of the company until the closing.
- No surprises in terms of new information emerging that could adversely affect the value of the company.
- Negotiation and signature by the parties of a mutually satisfactory SPA.
- The company must continue to deliver results according to budget until closing.

> The bottom line is that the only time you really know you've got a deal is when the money is in your bank account.

The bottom line is that the only time you really know you've got a deal is when the money is in your bank account. Nevertheless, investors will be considerably more careful in making a binding offer than a nonbinding offer, as the potential legal liability of a binding offer is much higher.

## EXCLUSIVITY

There is often friction between the investor and the target company over the issue of exclusivity. It is generally in the investor's interests to obtain exclusivity as soon as possible in the sale process in order to eliminate any competition. A typical investor argument for exclusivity is the substantial advisory fees incurred by moving forward with the Transaction (not to mention internal management resources), which he or she is unwilling to commit unless exclusivity is granted. Investors may claim, with some legitimacy, that it would be a waste of resources in the event that they followed through in good faith, and then you decide to sell to someone else.

It is generally in your interests, as owner, to postpone the granting of exclusivity in order to preserve competition, or at least the possibility of competition, for as long as possible. You will be in a very strong position to resist calls for exclusivity when you are negotiating simultaneously with three or four potentially serious investors. You are typically better off letting one bidder drop out of the process and having two or three remaining strong bidders, than granting exclusivity to that one bidder, unless, of course, that bidder is by far the most serious, and is willing to commit to a very generous valuation, up front.

Ultimately, whether or not exclusivity is granted boils down to the relative strength of the positions of the parties and their ability to negotiate. If a private equity firm tells you they never participate in competitive processes, because in a competitive process it's sometimes the party who makes a mistake in the valuation who wins the deal, it may be a perfectly rational decision to give it exclusivity, particularly if there are no other investors on the horizon. Don't make that decision too hastily, though: make sure you and your advisors have adequately canvassed the field of potential investors. After all, is it a mistake if an investor is willing to give you a higher multiple, or ascribe more synergistic value to your company? These are judgment calls.

## TRANSACTION STRUCTURING

It is quite seldom that a deal is concluded based on what you requested in the Process Letter, or on the basis of the first offer made by the investor. Once you select an investor who is also ready to proceed with a definitive SPA, you both may explore alternative Transaction structures, and this final structure may be the result of a protracted negotiation.

How a deal is ultimately structured will depend on a number of factors, including assets and liabilities being acquired, tax considerations, and third party consents (e.g. banks). There are three main types of Transaction structures: (a) share purchase; (b) asset purchase; and (c) merger.

> Sometimes Due Diligence reveals an unexpected skeleton, or one that was larger than expected.

While most sellers start the sale process seeking a share purchase, sometimes the parties agree that an asset purchase is preferable. For one thing, it may entail a more beneficial tax treatment for one or both parties. Secondly, it greatly reduces the need for Due Diligence on the part of the investor. Whenever an investor buys shares, there is always a fear of purchasing unknown liabilities. What skeleton in the closet did the investors miss? Sometimes Due Diligence reveals an unexpected skeleton, or one that was larger than expected, in which case the investors lose confidence and insist on an asset purchase. An asset purchase will also make it simpler for an investor to purchase specific lines of business or assets, without having to buy the entire business.

Under a merger, two or more legal entities will typically fuse into one entity. In most jurisdictions, the remaining entity will be the legal successor of both entities that were merged. Hence there is no legal discontinuity. In some jurisdictions, courts may deem an asset purchase to be a merger. In this case, the purchaser needs to be careful as they may end up also owning the seller's liabilities. If you are considering a purchase, hire competent legal counsel and exercise due care.

Whether a Transaction occurs by way of share purchase, asset purchase, or merger, it is important to understand how payments may be structured:

- *Escrow:* Investors will usually want a percentage of the purchase price to be paid into an escrow account (normally held by a legal advisor, bank, or other reputable and independent third party). The escrow amount is one of the most fiercely negotiated aspects of a Transaction: it may be in the range of 0 to 25 percent or more of the Transaction price, and be held for a duration of one to three years, or more. The escrow amount is typically designed to back up the Representations and Warranties given by the sellers in the SPA.
- *Deferred compensation:* Is the deal an all-cash deal, or could the seller finance a part of the compensation by way of a promissory note? Is there any security for a promissory note (e.g., mortgage on real estate of the company or guarantee provided by the investor)?
- *Share compensation:* Will the investor offer, and will the seller accept any share compensation in the investor's entity? If so, what will be the valuation? If the investor is a public entity, will there be any lock-up period (e.g., period during which such shares cannot be sold, as prescribed by stock exchanges)?
- *Earn-Out:* The concept of an **Earn-Out** is very simple, yet its proper execution is fiendishly difficult. An Earn-Out is a Transaction where a portion of the proceeds is paid after closing, in a manner that depends on the performance of the acquired company, judged most likely by its earnings. Often Earn-Outs are used in owner-managed companies, and generally require that the seller remains in the management of the company in question to ensure that performance targets and a smooth transition are achieved. Earn-Outs are becoming increasingly popular.

Business owners usually have more confidence in the future performance of their companies than prospective buyers do.

Business owners usually have more confidence in the future performance of their companies than prospective buyers do. You will most likely have emotional attachments to your business and perhaps a better understanding of the risks, whereas a potential buyer will tend to place more emphasis on possible downsides associated with an acquisition. This discrepancy may sometimes be quite large, resulting in a valuation deadlock. The investor may then graciously agree to break the standstill by improving an initially conservative offer, but on condition that you actualize the Business Plan or level of performance promised. It is a perfectly natural reaction for an investor or buyer to decide to share the upside with the seller, as it creates a strong motivation for the selling shareholders to remain involved with and maximize the performance of the company. This helps minimize transition risk for the buyer. It also helps the investor lock in the owner of the company for an orderly transition.

Yet the implementation of Earn-Outs remains devilishly difficult, primarily because of five factors.

1.  It is tricky to set the performance benchmarks that should be achieved, such as determining if the Earn-Out should be tied to revenue, operating margins, profit, or a combination of these benchmarks. The sellers should have an excellent Business Plan or budget that gives a relatively accurate estimate of future performance, or else the Earn-Out can become meaningless. Establishing performance benchmarks can be the subject of protracted negotiations, with each change in benchmark potentially impacting valuation.

    There are issues of control. Compensation of the sellers is tied to performance, but under Earn-Outs, operating control is usually ceded to the buyers. Hence, there must be an elaborate system of checks and balances, usually in the form of veto rights that give at least a degree of operational autonomy to the sellers (who remain in management). They would be foolish to accept deferred compensation if they had no control over the conditions in which the Earn-Out might be achieved.

2.  It may be difficult to accommodate unanticipated events during the Earn-Out period, such as what happens if the business plan changes for whatever reason, if an unanticipated capital injection is required, or if a *force majeure* occurs. It is simply impossible to anticipate every eventuality in a contract.

3.  It is difficult to account for the synergies between the buyer's and the seller's companies, which raises questions like what happens if the buyer brings new orders to the seller's company. The buyer might feel that the seller is achieving a windfall when benchmarks are being achieved

even if the seller is delivering less than promised. These issues must be carefully discussed, as it is important to avoid misunderstandings.

4. Sellers will typically want to protect themselves against fraudulent or arbitrary actions by buyers aimed at short-changing them on their Earn-Out proceeds. As with any form of deferred compensation, there may be temptation on the part of the buyers to find a justified or unjustified pretext for deducting from those proceeds.

> As a rule, drafting an SPA requires a high degree of legal sophistication; drafting an Earn-Out takes the level of sophistication even higher.

As a rule, drafting an SPA requires a high degree of legal sophistication; drafting an Earn-Out takes the level of sophistication even higher. Legal fees may increase due to the number of hours taken as well as higher-than-normal billing rates for top-notch legal counsel. Even the best laid plans, however, may go awry. For example, those sellers who negotiated an Earn-Out prior to a recession or cyclical downturn will need to work exceedingly hard to achieve targets that were established when times were still good.

Earn-outs merit serious consideration when structuring Transactions. They are not for neophytes: both buyer and seller should have at least one or two people on their respective teams who have structured at least half a dozen Earn-Outs. While there is enormous potential to create a genuine win-win solution between buyer and seller, there is also potential for disaster.

## HEADS OF AGREEMENT

At one or more times during a sale process, seller and investor may wish to clarify their understanding of the commercial terms of a Transaction prior to proceeding further in the process (e.g., prior to launching a Due Diligence process or commencing the negotiation of an SPA). This purpose may be satisfied by a Heads of Agreement, Heads of Terms, or Term Sheet; for the sake of simplicity, I will stick with the expression Term Sheet.

A Term Sheet is an optional feature of a sale process. It may be particularly useful in a complex Transaction to first negotiate a Term Sheet so as to see the forest from the trees (e.g., have agreement as to the main parameters of a deal) prior to negotiating the SPA. In such situations, it may streamline the negotiation process and save the parties time and money.

> It makes sense to set out the main terms and conditions of a possible
> Transaction prior to granting exclusivity.

It makes sense to set out the main terms and conditions of a possible
Transaction prior to granting exclusivity. Once you grant exclusivity, some
investors may be tempted to find issues that require a downward negotiation of price. A Term Sheet could be used to establish a clear price expectation, and may, for example, contain a clause stating that any attempt by
the investor to reduce the price may release you, the seller, from any obligation pertaining to exclusivity.

One advantage of negotiating a Term Sheet is that the parties may negotiate the commercial terms of a Transaction without the presence of legal
advisors, which could save a considerable amount in legal fees. Some would
argue that legal advisors have no role meddling with commercial terms in
any event! It is always a good idea, however, to have your legal advisor review
the Term Sheet (or any other agreement to be signed during a sale process)
prior to the actual execution of the agreement between the parties. A Term
Sheet can be either binding or nonbinding. It's a judgment call so consult
your legal advisor as to what would be best in your particular situation.

## SALE AND PURCHASE AGREEMENT

The definitive agreement governing the sale and purchase of a company is
generally the SPA. This can be a document of tens or even hundreds of
pages. To provide a definitive and exhaustive description of all the points
that should be covered such an Agreement is beyond the scope of this book.
Instead, let's look at some of the more general concepts:

- *Purchase price and Transaction structuring:* The SPA sets out the purchase price and the Transaction structuring. It may call for multiple
  closings (e.g., under an Earn-Out) and prescribe the timing, nature of
  compensation, and type of compensation payable at each closing.
- *Representations and Warranties:* This is often the most contentious
  part of the negotiation of the SPA. Investors will sometimes start from
  the premise that the sellers should be personally liable, jointly and
  severally, for any error, omission, or misrepresentation, and should be
  subject to repaying the entire purchase price or beyond. In the case of
  this extreme position, you should ask the investor why he or she both-
  ered to conduct Due Diligence and hire advisors, if the entire burden

is being thrust back onto you, the seller. You could limit your Representations and Warranties by:

- *Putting a cap on representations and warranties:* For example, total representations and warranties to which you might be subject should not exceed a pre-defined percentage of purchase price. Otherwise, you might find yourself having to pay out more in representations and warranties than the purchase price you receive for the business.
- *Not having joint and several liability:* If Shareholder A owns 80 percent of the company being sold, while B and C each own 10 percent, it is absurd to expect B and C to cover all of the representations and warranties to be offered by the sellers. In my experience, most investors will settle for each seller taking a pro rata share of the Representations and Warranties.
- *Narrowing the scope of the Representations and Warranties:* Instead of providing blanket Representations and Warranties (e.g., that all information provided in the IM is true and complete), as the seller, you could seek to limit your liability by limiting both the scope and duration of the Representations and Warranties. For example, for issues pertaining to taxation, limit the duration to two or three years, and even then, allow Representations and Warranties only in the event that it is the tax authorities that initiate proceedings.

Unfortunately most courts will not accept the defense of: "Honest, Judge, I told the investor about the problem over dinner one night". It is in your own interests to have these issues covered in writing, with the advice of competent counsel. The negotiation of Representations and Warranties is the most demanding part of the sale process for legal advisors. There are few things that make me sweat more in a Transaction than when a legal advisor is out of his or her depth in negotiating Representations and Warranties (and the SPA in general).

> There are few things that make me sweat more in a Transaction than when a legal advisor is out of his or her depth in negotiating Representations and Warranties.

- *Material adverse change (MAC):* Many SPAs will contain what is known as a MAC clause. The MAC clause typically states that in the event of a material adverse change to the business, between the time of signing the SPA and the closing, the investor shall have the right to

## BOX 9.3   EXAMPLE OF ARBITRATION OVER A MAC CLAUSE

In 2000, I was an expert witness at the London Court of International Arbitration, retained by a U.S. investor who had entered into an SPA to sell a Polish telecommunications firm. One hour prior to closing, the investor withdrew from the Transaction, alleging a MAC.

My role, as expert witness, was to examine the evidence (e.g., growth in number of lines, revenues, etc.) and determine whether there had, indeed, been a MAC. The arbitration panel accepted the conclusion of my report, that there wasn't a MAC, whereupon as expert witness my opinion was sought on the subject of my client's damages. My client was awarded and collected $39 million (in addition to keeping the investor's deposit of $10 million).

A MAC clause cannot be exercised at random by an investor. Nevertheless, it is better to avoid litigation or arbitration, which can easily cost hundreds of thousands of dollars.

withdraw from the Transaction, without penalty. In Anglo-Saxon jurisdictions, there is well-developed case law as to what constitutes a MAC (see Box 9.3).

- *Dispute resolution:* SPAs typically go into considerable detail concerning venues and procedures for dispute resolution. Should disputes go to arbitration, to what arbitration body should they go, according to what laws and in what language should the dispute be remedied? Should there be a *de minimis* provision (e.g., below a certain minimum amount, disputes would not be litigated or arbitrated)?
- *Price adjustment mechanisms:* Investors will almost always do their best to ensure that they receive that which they bargained for at closing. They may require financial statements to be prepared as of the closing date. Most likely closing will be scheduled for the end of a year, quarter, or month, when statements would be prepared in any event. Investors may try to establish minimum parameters for those matters that are important for them (e.g., shareholders' equity, working capital, inventory, or cash), as of the closing date. In the event that the parameter is not satisfied at closing, there may be a purchase price adjustment. Sellers may try to specify that conversely, if the parameter is exceeded, the purchase price adjustment will be in their favor. It boils down to a negotiation between the parties.

Negotiating purchase price adjustments, and defining them well, is one of the most important functions of accountants for each side during the negotiation of the SPA.

Negotiating purchase price adjustments, and defining them well, is one of the most important functions of accountants for each side during the negotiation of the SPA. The definition of the purchase price adjustment mechanism sometimes requires one or more fairly extensive appendices to the SPA. Often, the same accountants will be involved in monitoring the business for the purpose of calculating any purchase price adjustment. Alternatively, the parties may decide to appoint an independent third party as accountant.

- *Noncompete agreement:* Almost every investor will ask you, as the business owner, to sign a non-compete agreement. This is very difficult to avoid. Where there is considerable room for discussion, however, is on the subject of scope and duration. Duration is typically anywhere from one to several years. Scope refers to the narrowness or breadth of the definition of excluded activities. For example, if you are the owner of an IT firm, should you be excluded from working in the IT business? If your company was focused on CRM systems, arguably the non-compete should apply only to these. Also, how narrowly or broadly do you define the scope of the non-compete agreement in the geographic sense?
- *Conditions of closing:* What conditions must be satisfied prior to closing?
- Approval of the banks of the new owner (most bank loans have change of control provisions).
- Approval of the competition office or regulatory authorities, if necessary.
- Curing defects in title to one or more assets, and so on.
- Signing of additional contracts (e.g., new employment contract for company management), Shareholders' Agreement, and so on.

It is generally the legal advisor's responsibility to drive the agenda for satisfaction of conditions and then to arrange the closing, where a myriad of documents are signed, evidence of ownership (e.g., shares) passes to the investor, and cash passes to the seller.

Time is your enemy. Once you have the idea, and you are agreed, then get it done.

The negotiation of SPAs is often a marathon business, frequently running right through the night. In addition to technical competence and negotiation prowess, they require patience, endurance, and stamina. Just because you sign an SPA doesn't mean that the deal is done and you can sit back. I've seen some owners become complacent when the SPA has been signed (or even when the Term Sheet has been signed). The number of deals that unravel after the signature of an SPA and before closing is surprising. Perhaps a new skeleton jumps out of the closet, a MAC appears, an important client or staff member is lost, and so on. You should remain vigilant; do not relax your pace toward closing the Transaction until the money is in your bank account. As the CEO of an American company stated: "Time is your enemy. Once you have the idea, and you are agreed, then get it done."[1]

Part of the reason time is against you is that there can be so many intervening events: key staff leaving, major fluctuations in currency exchanges, a fire in your facility, a change of circumstances with the investor, or a meltdown of financial markets (see Box 9.4). Each of these events may trigger a renegotiation or may prove to be a deal-breaker. By minimizing the number of conditions to closing, and by trying to resolve those issues as quickly as possible, you will improve the chances of your Transaction closing.

---

### BOX 9.4 9/11 FOILS TRANSACTION

In 2001, Euro-Phoenix was involved in a major telecommunications Transaction. When binding offers came in, there was a gap of approximately €20 million between the highest offer and what our client was prepared to accept. Over time, and through tough negotiations, the gap was reduced to €5 million. The parties were starting to become quite optimistic about closing.

Then on September 11, two hijacked aircraft hit the World Trade Center, while another hit the Pentagon. Financial markets the world over tumbled. As a result of the events on 9/11, the gap once again returned to €20 million. According to the investors, higher perceptions of risk and depressed stock markets justified their position. The negotiations failed. The company was sold five years later, to a different investor, this time Euro-Phoenix acting for the investor.

## CLOSING THE TRANSACTION

The SPA should describe in considerable detail the events that must transpire on the closing date. How will payment be made (bank account details, etc.)? What evidence of payment must be given prior to ownership of shares passing to the investor? Does inventory need to be taken on the closing date? How will events be communicated to staff and the external world on the closing date? Will a press release be necessary?

> It helps to have banks that are cooperative and prepared to act quickly on the closing date, to make transfers and provide evidence of transfers having been made.

A closing typically lasts from a few hours to a full day. There are often dozens or hundreds of documents to be signed, which are sometimes held in escrow until funds change hands. It may take one or two days for the funds to be transferred, and documents transferring title should not be released until funds have been received. Evidence of completion of all conditions to closing must be provided by both parties. It helps to have banks that are cooperative and prepared to act quickly on the closing date, to make transfers and provide evidence of transfers having been made.

Closings are sometimes so complex, with so many parties and issues to manage, that legal advisors may go through a pre-closing, a kind of a dress rehearsal, to make sure they are on the same page when they come to closing.

## NONCOMPETITIVE PROCESSES

There may be certain situations where a noncompetitive process might be more appropriate than a competitive process. First, an investor may put such an attractive offer on the table that as the owner you decide to forego other negotiations. Second, an investor may insist that there not be a competitive process, for whatever reason (e.g., they are not prepared to engage advisors and undertake the effort of Due Diligence unless they have exclusivity).

If you come across either of these situations, ask yourself the following questions:

- How sure are you that the offer you have received is truly exceptional (especially if you have not yet received competing offers or a valuation)?
- What is the opportunity cost of your time? How much of a setback will it be if you spend several months negotiating with one party, and the negotiations fall through for whatever reason?
- What is the opportunity cost in terms of passing up other potential investors? Have other parties been identified? If so, have they expressed any valuation range? Will they still be around and interested in negotiating in several months time?

Should you grant any party exclusivity, give careful consideration to the duration of the exclusivity. You may want to pin them down on a written valuation (e.g., in the form of a Term Sheet), and even stipulate that in the event that they attempt to reduce the valuation, the exclusivity may automatically expire.

# CHAPTER 10

# Negotiating a Transaction

*Start out with an ideal and end up with a deal.*
—Karl Albrecht (b. 1920)
German entrepreneur, founder of Aldi

The sale of a company is typically not one negotiation, but a series of negotiations, from negotiating the Confidentiality Agreement to negotiating the **Term Sheet** and then the **Sale and Purchase Agreement** (**SPA**). There are often unexpected negotiations mid-course as well: perhaps your company doesn't meet the budget, or there is a currency exchange fluctuation or loss of a contract which changes the value of your company. Negotiation is therefore one of the key competencies required for any **Transaction**, crucial for mergers and acquisitions (M&A) professionals. And yet, at times, I am shocked at how much money people leave on the table, simply through being unaware of, or not practicing, basic negotiation techniques (see Box 10.1).

This chapter covers some of the following very basic negotiation principles:

> At times, I am shocked at how much money people leave on the table, simply through being unaware of, or not practicing, basic negotiation techniques

- Get to know your negotiating partner
- Let your negotiating partner make the first offer
- Concede in small increments
- After asking a crucial question, hold your tongue

---

**BOX 10.1   NEGOTIATING EXAMPLE**

Euro-Phoenix once negotiated alongside a client who had never before negotiated a Transaction, and was very emotional by nature. We spent quite a few hours briefing him on the negotiation strategy for the SPA, and even drew up a written memorandum as to an agreed negotiation strategy.

When the negotiations commenced, our client kept thinking that by capitulating to one request of the investor, the parties could shake hands on a deal, and the deal would be concluded. The investor, however, sensing our client's emotion and agitation, kept coming back with more and more requests. Each time our client capitulated or compromised, this emboldened the investor to make more requests.

Finally, we came to an agreement with our client that we, as his financial advisors, would represent him in the negotiations. We succeeded in clawing back some of what had been earlier capitulated, but had to draw a line in the sand on five or six of the most contentious points, stating that any concession beyond this point would be a deal-breaker. The investor, fortunately, accepted.

---

- Every term of the deal also depends on every other term
- Be prepared to walk away from the deal
- Know your best alternative

The above principles sound so very simple, and yet are so difficult to implement in practice. When I have taught negotiations in the past, whether MBA students or seasoned businessmen, even if I tell the class the principles before the case study negotiations, inevitably the majority of participants still violate more than one of these principles, behavioral patterns are so deeply ingrained.

## GET TO KNOW YOUR NEGOTIATING PARTNER

Ask lots of questions. What makes your investors tick? Why do they want to invest in your company in particular? What are their emotional drivers? What are their thoughts on the timing of the Transaction? Have they made any acquisitions in the past? (If so, you might find out their valuations.) What is their internal decision-making structure? Who really calls the shots?

This information will help ensure that you are dealing with the real decision-makers when appropriate, assess their real motivations, and propose solutions that cater to their needs.

Ask yourself also whether this is the type of person or investor to whom you'd want to entrust your company.

## LET YOUR NEGOTIATING PARTNER MAKE THE FIRST OFFER

Always, without fail, seek to encourage your negotiating partner to make the first offer on any particular issue. This often brings surprising results. Your negotiating partner, for example, might value your company at more than what you thought it was possibly worth. This is perfectly consistent with our typical practice of no asking price: the nature of a competitive process puts the investor in the position of needing to make the first offer.

If you must make the first offer, make it at the highest end of the defensible spectrum.

If, for example, purchase price is what you are negotiating, then start with the highest price you could conceivably defend for the sale of your company. Don't be shy! It is a classic error in negotiations to be painted into a corner where you make a first offer that is too low.

## CONCEDE IN SMALL INCREMENTS

If you concede in large increments, your negotiating partner will sense a capitulation. By conceding in small and even smaller increments as you go along, your negotiating partner will get the signal that there is not that much room for negotiation.

## AFTER ASKING A CRUCIAL QUESTION, HOLD YOUR TONGUE

Silence is uncomfortable. It creates a vacuum and nature abhors a vacuum. It also puts pressure on the party to whom the question was directed to answer. Many times, after I ask a key question of the investor (e.g., "how much would you be prepared to pay for my client's company?", or a similarly pointed question), and there is a long silence while the investor is thinking about the answer, I have seen my own clients discomfited. For whatever reason, they choose to fill the vacuum and answer the question. This takes the pressure off the investor, we miss a chance of obtaining crucial information, and the client signals that he might be overly anxious.

A friend of mine, also an M&A advisor, developed a habit of stomping on a particular client's foot whenever his client spoke out of turn. In his enthusiasm to keep his client quiet, on one occasion he accidently broke his client's toe! I'm certainly not advocating physical violence, but this anecdote drives home the importance of staying silent at critical junctures.

## EVERY TERM OF THE DEAL ALSO
## DEPENDS ON EVERY OTHER TERM

There are dozens, if not hundreds, of points that must be negotiated in an M&A Transaction: price, scheduling of payments, **Representations and Warranties**, salary packages, and non-compete agreements, to name but a few. For example, stricter Representations and Warranties will require a higher price, and vice versa. So do not get boxed in by agreeing to a certain price, only to find that the investor is negotiating an excessively stiff set of Representations and Warranties. You can use these techniques for each of the many points to be negotiated in the course of selling your company.

> If you apply the negotiation techniques well, but fundamentally misjudge the investor's character, you may win the negotiation battle (i.e., close your deal), but lose the war.

Negotiating techniques will take you part, but not all of the way, in negotiating the sale of your company. These techniques are little tricks of the trade that help you improve price, terms, and conditions. But one question you should ask yourself even before applying these techniques is whether this is an investor to whom you would entrust your company. Could you incur reputational risks by conducting a Transaction with a particular investor? Is he or she likely to honor contractual agreements, such as for deferred payment? Is he or she likely to be litigious, for example on Representations and Warranties? If you apply the negotiation techniques well, but fundamentally misjudge the investor's character, you may win the negotiation battle (i.e., close your deal), but lose the war.

## BE PREPARED TO WALK AWAY FROM THE DEAL

Investors will almost always see if they can get better prices or terms. If you show flexibility or willingness to consider, they will push you for concessions. And if you grant those concessions (especially if you grant them quickly), they may very well conclude that more concessions may be possible. Some investors will keep pushing for concessions until you tell them directly that any further pressure is a deal-breaker. That does not mean you always need to dig in your heels and insist that there is no flexibility. You don't want to acquire a reputation for being inflexible, which may harm the negotiation. It's a judgment call as to when you dig in your heels, and when you entertain the possibility of flexibility. Ironically, if you make a first offer that is too low, you may leave yourself very little room to go lower, thereby acquiring a reputation for inflexibility.

## KNOW YOUR BEST ALTERNATIVE

Fisher *et al.*[1] developed a concept known as BATNA: Best Alternative To a Negotiated Agreement. For example, if you have an offer on the table for the sale of your company for $32 million, and you have another one on the table for $28 million, in the event that the investor who offered $32 million tries to bring the price down to $25 million after **Due Diligence,** under no circumstances should you accept less than $28 million, everything else being equal. This is one of the big advantages of a competitive process: a multitude of offers will give you a clear and quantified BATNA. Your BATNA helps you define where you draw the line in being prepared to walk away from a potential investor.

Your BATNA might be another competing offer, or the likely compensation from another exit method (e.g., **Management Buyout [MBO]** or **Intergenerational Transfer**).

A seller will usually have a BATNA below which he should refuse to go (i.e. he will not sell for less than $28 million); a buyer should have a BATNA above which he should not be prepared to go (i.e. he might not be prepared to go higher than $35 million). In such a case, the only factor that determines where the price ends up—between $28 million and $38 million— is the relative negotiating ability of the two parties. I hope you are persuaded that your negotiating ability, and that of your advisors, can make the difference of millions of dollars when buying or selling a company.

In conclusion, negotiation skill can make a difference of many millions of dollars in negotiating Transactions. Unless you are an extremely strong negotiator, and able to keep your cool in tense situations, you may wish to consider putting someone else in the front line of negotiation, perhaps someone who is an even stronger negotiator than yourself. Ultimately, the person in the front line will still need to seek approval from you. Having the front line negotiator defer to a higher authority is a way of avoiding costly negotiating mistakes, such as conceding too much or an omission to deal with a certain issue.

# CHAPTER 11

# Cross-border Transactions

*The notion of the world as a village is becoming a reality.*
—James Wolfensohn (b. 1933)
9th President of the World Bank

**G**lobally, according to statistics from Mergermarket, over the past decade approximately 55 to 65 percent of **Transactions** were cross-border Transactions. (Calculations done by Euro-Phoenix based on Mergermarket statistics.) This is simply too important a segment of the market to ignore.

> When selling your company, you have the choice of canvassing investors in your home market, in your region, or globally.

When selling your company, you have the choice of canvassing investors in your home market, in your region, or globally. I can't see any downside to opening up your marketing efforts to international marketing, and there is certainly a very big upside: you have the potential to attract more investors, which leads to more competition, hence a potentially higher price and better terms for you as the seller. Is it any wonder that cross-border Transactions are growing so rapidly? You probably wouldn't try to sell a small company doing $2–$3 million of revenue on the other side of the planet. The cost/benefit for both the seller and the buyer would not be there in most instances. But for a business doing $20–$30 million in revenue, it could be worthwhile for an investor to come from a different part of the world.

This chapter does not aim to teach the reader to become a cross-cultural expert or to provide an inventory of cultural differences between different nationalities. I merely try to recount a number of episodes that should heighten the reader's awareness to the need for sensitivity to cultural differences to avoid miscommunication.

## WHY DON'T MORE PEOPLE MARKET THEIR COMPANIES INTERNATIONALLY?

It boils down to lack of familiarity: familiarity with investors, with language, with culture. Have you ever tried getting through the switchboard of a Chinese company? Unless you are conversant in Mandarin, it's almost hopeless.

The cross-cultural aspects of international negotiations can also be daunting (see Box 11.1). Horror stories abound:

- In Albania, I thought my negotiations were faring badly. My Albanian interpreter kept shaking his head. It was quite unsettling; I couldn't figure out what I was doing wrong. As it turned out, in Albania, and in a number of other Balkan countries, shaking your head is an affirmative gesture. Conversely, nodding your head up and down is how you say no!
- In China, in a negotiations workshop, I asked two people to negotiate something in a role play. Both of them, and indeed, the whole room, came to a standstill. You could hear a pin drop for what seemed like an eternity. I had made the mistake of asking someone senior to negotiate with someone more junior, and in a society concerned with losing face, that was a show-stopper.
- In Japan, I sneezed quite loudly during a negotiation in the lobby of a very elegant Tokyo hotel. What had been a bustling, busy, loud environment became completely silent for a pregnant moment. It was only much later that I realized that sneezing in Japan is considered a barbaric act, like spitting is for Europeans or Americans.
- Of course, in Japan, your hosts will never say no. The average Westerner will typically interpret yes as meaning agreement, whereas in Japan it's basically not much more than an acknowledgement: "yes, I heard you". You can imagine how many Western businessmen thought the deal was done, when in fact they were merely being acknowledged.

As Geert Hofstede, one of the seminal thinkers on the subject of cross-cultural differences, wrote: "...people carry 'mental programs' that are developed in the family in early childhood and reinforced in schools and

## BOX 11.1   A SPECTACULAR EXAMPLE OF CULTURE CLASH

In 1996, while with the World Bank, I advised the Government of Togo on the divestiture of its crown jewel, the national phosphate mines. We had conducted a competitive tender among major international investment banks. The highest score was obtained by Wasserstein Perella & Co., an investment banking firm based in New York. We invited it to negotiate a contract.

The Government of Togo (or at least the Government officials I was dealing with) had never hired a major investment banking firm, and they had never before seen a sophisticated, U.S.-style investment banking contract. They spoke French and little or poor English. You can imagine the culture shock for both sides when the Wasserstein Perella team arrived, speaking no French, and with a 50-page draft contract that had more than 10 pages of **Representations and Warranties** to be provided by the Government. After the initial shock of the draft contract, via translation, it was not possible for the two sides to loosen up and develop a normal social relationship.

Despite several weeks of trying to bring the two sides to agreement, it became apparent that even if a contract were signed, the cultural gap was simply too large, and that it would be nearly impossible for the parties to develop a normal working relationship. Hence the runner-up in the competitive bidding process was invited to negotiate a contract. Within days of arrival, a contract was concluded with a major Paris-based investment banking firm. Not only could it communicate in the same language, it was prepared to accept the draft contract template of the World Bank as a point of departure.

organizations, and [...] these mental programs contain a component of national culture."[1] He defines culture as "the collective programming of the mind".[2]

One dimension that I find crucial in the negotiation context is the length of time it takes to build enough trust to really do business.

## THE CHALLENGES OF CROSS CULTURAL NEGOTIATIONS

One dimension that I find crucial in the negotiation context is the length of time it takes to build enough trust to really do business. Unlike in the United States, where you can sit down with a total stranger and begin structuring a deal, in some countries you might build a relationship for a year or more before seriously talking business. This happened to me in Ukraine: I was getting nowhere in a negotiation with an ex-Soviet army general. He was being evasive and beating around the bush, until after we had been trying to do business for over a year, he invited me to his home, where we each consumed 13 ounces of vodka before he offered me the hand of his daughter. Then, and only then, could we get down to really doing business!

> You also need to think outside the box and be prepared to interpret things differently than you might interpret them at home.

Cultures can and will vary dramatically. I don't read up on the culture of a country before going there for a business negotiation. But I do go into cross-cultural negotiations acutely aware that there might be huge differences in areas that could be very surprising. You really have to have your wits about you to not give off signals that might be received the wrong way. You also need to think outside the box and be prepared to interpret things differently than you might interpret them at home.

Someone once said to me, in a thick Canadian-Hungarian accent: "Les, you are a great liar." Thankfully I didn't fly off the handle at the perceived insult; as it turned out, he was trying to tell me that I was a great lawyer! When on unfamiliar territory, suppress your impulse to react quickly. Find a measured response.

One of the challenges in cross-cultural negotiations is finding the right balance of politeness, respect, and deference. Even politicians at the highest level do not always get it right: You may remember the incident where President Obama bowed deeply—some would say too deeply—to the Japanese Emperor. Different languages and cultures have different ways of expressing politeness. For example, most languages have a polite form for the word you (*vous* in French or *usted* in Spanish) or an everyday, not-so-polite version of the word (*tu* in French and Spanish). Some languages (e.g., Hungarian) even have three degrees of politeness. English, from this point of view, is a very democratic language, and has only one form of you. This simplifies life tremendously, but as a consequence, English native speakers often have a very difficult time adjusting to other languages. Whoever would have thought that French, a modern European language, would have an archaic flourish for finishing letters: *Je vous prie de bien vouloir agreér, Monsieur, l'expression de mes sentiments distingués* which translates loosely as "I ask you kindly to accept, Sir, the assurance of my highest consideration".[3]

So coming back to you as a business owner, and how this ties into selling your business. If you intend to sell your business to an investor next door or in the same country, a local advisory team will do. But if you are open to the possibility of marketing your company internationally, then you should also be seeking related competencies from your advisory team members. Have they negotiated many cross-border Transactions? Do they have the necessary cross-cultural skills? Does your financial advisor have the kind of international networks that would lend themselves to cross-border Transactions?

# Conclusion

# The Only Question with Wealth Is, What Do You Do with It?

I hope you have enjoyed this exploration of **Business Exit Planning** and **Transaction Management**. I would like to wrap up this book with three subjects:

- First, I revisit the three overarching themes as explored in the Introduction, to drive the points home.
- If you are successful in your **Transaction**, you are likely to have an inordinate amount of cash on your hands, perhaps more than you have ever had in your life. I offer a few suggestions on how to prepare for this.
- Finally, I talk about some of the potential macroeconomic implications from a lack of succession or exit planning. These are not isolated incidents. I suggest they are macroeconomically significant.

## REVISITING THE THREE OVERARCHING THEMES

Do you recall the three overarching themes of this book that I outlined in the Introduction?

1. A **Business Exit** should not be a spontaneous process, but the result of careful planning.
2. Business owners tend to underestimate what it takes to exit.
3. There is often a mismatch in negotiating strength between business owners and professional investors.

You may not be able to formulate a definitive opinion on any of the three subjects until you have closed at least one Transaction. But now that we've been through the process, in theory, you will be better prepared and more successful when you do start your exit process.

## The Need for Preparation and a Systematic Approach

Luck is where preparation meets opportunity

While it may be theoretically possible to be lucky and sell your business using an ad hoc approach, I have only seen a handful of such incidents in the last 25 years, and all of these were in markets where there was irrational exuberance. You may have heard the expression: luck is where preparation meets opportunity. It is seldom a total accident. The more you prepare, in the form of Business Exit Planning and Transaction Management, the more you are increasing the odds in your favor.

A competitive process will unleash the full power of the market. Unless you have a competitive process, you will never know whether you got the best possible deal, not just pricewise, but in satisfying every other objective, whether it is finding an investor with synergies or one who is likely to take your company to new heights.

A competitive process, in turn, requires thorough preparation, at every level, from the **Information Memorandum (IM)** to the **Data Room**. Otherwise, you will not be in a position to handle the incredible intensity of the **Due Diligence** process with multiple investors, simultaneously.

## Underestimation of the Level of Effort Required to Successfully Exit

Now that you've almost finished reading this book, you should have a firmer grasp of the myriad of competencies required for a successful exit, as well as the intensity of the activity. Performing a Business Exit Planning process in six months or less, or a Transaction in nine months or less, it is truly a marathon. The Due Diligence process and negotiation of the **Sale and Purchase Agreement (SPA)** represent two sprints at the end of the marathon. This tests the endurance even of high-energy performers. And, don't forget, all the activities we've discussed that pertain to Business Exit Planning and the Transaction itself must be carried out alongside the day-to-day activities of conducting your normal business.

By the time an investor enters the Due Diligence phase, chances are that he or she has been supplied with a forecast of your company's performance for the coming year. Often the forecast is broken down by month. The investor will usually base any non-binding or binding offer on your company achieving its forecast during the months prior to closing. And these months are the most intense months of the sale process. Where there is a significant deviation, you may well be facing a renegotiation in price. I've seen company management so tied up with the sale process that it neglects the running of the business, so that as a result, the forecast is not achieved. You have to keep your eye on the ball at all times, both operationally and with respect to the Transaction.

## Mismatch in Negotiation Strength

It's a given that as a business owner you will know your industry, related technologies, markets, and so on, at least as well as any potential investor. But now that you've read this book, you realize that many broader, multi-disciplinary competencies are required: legal, valuation, taxation, running a sale process, setting up a Data Room, writing an IM, negotiating with investors, and so on. It is not just the theoretical knowledge of the subject matter, but also the practical experience that comes from successfully having closed numerous Transactions in the past.

There are really only two ways you can compensate for this mismatch: hire the appropriate advisors with the necessary knowledge and experience, and prepare, prepare, prepare.

> You determine when you put your company on the market. It is amazing how many owners throw away the advantage of timing by putting their companies on the market without adequate preparation.

One of the big advantages you have as a business owner is that you determine when you put your company on the market. In other words, you can spend as much time as you like preparing your company, prior to going to market. Those who rush headlong into the sale process forego this advantage.

## YOU HAVE RAISED YOUR CASH. WHAT NEXT?

Most Transactions are celebrated with a closing dinner, usually at the invitation of the financial advisors. This could be an emotional moment for you, as you symbolically hand over the keys to the new owners. The emotions run the full gamut from the euphoria of cashing a huge check (and for once seeing money in your personal account, rather than in a corporate account), to a kind of post-partum depression about having let go of your baby.

It is important that by the time the closing dinner comes around, you, as a former business owner, are well on your way to transitioning on at least two fronts, even if you will be spending a good amount of time with the new owners assisting with the transition. First, you should be developing a strategy for what you will do with your time post-transition. Philanthropy, perhaps? Or starting another business? Or traveling? You should also be well on your way to deciding what you will do with the money. Have you diversified it appropriately? Do you have the necessary expertise to back you up, whether it is angel investing or purchasing shares?

> The psychological challenge of dealing with a windfall (albeit a hard-earned windfall) and a lot of spare time has defeated many a good man or woman.

Holding on to their hard-earned proceeds of divestiture, and growing it, proves to be more difficult than many business owners envisage. The psychological challenge of dealing with a windfall (albeit a hard-earned windfall) and a lot of spare time has defeated many a good man or woman. This could be because many business owners have been so focused on running their businesses that they have never really acquired a competency for investing, which is a completely different competency than running a business. As George Bernard Shaw once said: "The surest way to ruin a man who doesn't know how to handle money is to give him some."[1] A fundamental decision you will need to make is whether to manage your funds yourself or hire a professional asset manager or wealth management firm. Don't underestimate the challenge of transitioning from company CEO/owner to wealth manager.

Whichever option you choose, proper diversification of your portfolio should be the cornerstone of your strategy. First and foremost, your asset allocation should be between different classes of assets. Asset classes include, for example, equities, debt (also known as fixed income products), commodities (such as gold), real estate, cash, and so on. And then you should give some thought to diversification within a class of assets (e.g., what your weighting should be in sectors with respect to your equity portfolio). Equities typically perform well in times of economic stability and growth. Fixed income may still produce negative returns (e.g., if you are invested in bonds at a time of rapidly rising interest rates). Gold is considered an excellent hedge in a portfolio in times of instability. Geographic diversification is also becoming increasingly important. Asset allocation is said to account for more than 90 percent of the performance of a diversified portfolio.

Fundamental to your decisions about asset allocation are your investment goals, and in particular the degree of risk that you are prepared to take on. Asset allocation should reflect the level of risk that you are prepared to absorb. You should set objectives for your investment portfolio and develop a strategy for achieving your objectives. If you're not sure what you're doing, engage a professional wealth manager.

Choosing a professional wealth manager is an extremely difficult task. Although there might be a blue chip firm and brand behind him or her, it is the individual who is making the decisions. It generally takes five to 10 years for a wealth management firm to ascertain whether a freshly hired wealth manager is or is not performing.

An important part of your objectives, one which greatly impacts your strategy, is your time horizon. For example, if you are going to begin drawing down your savings in three or four years' time, you should not be placing too much reliance on equities, which are extremely volatile over the short term. Over the long term, a diversified portfolio of equities is likely to prove an excellent investment.

Whenever you invest your funds with an asset manager or wealth manager, you should ask whether they benchmark their performance against an index, such as the S&P 500. Every year stock goes up or down, so their performance can be quite objectively measured against the benchmark, and hence against their peers.

> If your manager is not even matching the benchmark, why are you paying him or her such high fees?

Typically fund managers will charge you a percentage of the portfolio (ranging from 1 to 2 percent of the value of the portfolio) for managing it. If your manager is not even matching the benchmark, why are you paying him or her such high fees? In such instances you will be better off buying an Index Fund (e.g., whose performance perfectly correlates to the index, such as the S&P 500). The average expenses of index-tracking mutual funds were 78 basis points (0.78 percent) per annum.[2] Alternatively, you might consider investing in a more recently created instrument, exchange-traded funds (ETFs): investment vehicles listed on public stock exchanges usually linked to a stock market index or asset class. In 2009, the average cost of U.S.-based ETFs was 31 basis points per annum.[3]

While my advice falls far short of a strategy, consider the following pointers when investing your portfolio:

- Seek the best possible professional advice early—months before closing your Transaction—about setting your objectives and an investment strategy.
- Properly diversify your portfolio, according to your strategy.
- Resist the temptation to go with stockbrokers or investment advisors who are peddling amazing deals, and stick to your strategy.
- Your strategy should be modified periodically, in light of possible changes in your investment objectives and possibly certain developments in the financial markets.

How do you make a small fortune investing your funds? Start off with a large fortune! Unfortunately, all too often, this joke becomes a reality.

## THE MACROECONOMIC EFFECTS OF SUCCESSION FAILURE

When we consider the weight in the economy of private, family-held businesses, we can only speculate as to the cost to society and the economy of a massive failure in succession planning, and businesses going bankrupt as a result. "The greatest part of America's wealth lies with family-owned businesses. Family firms comprise 80 percent to 90 percent of all business enterprises in North America. They contribute 64 percent of the GDP (over USD 5 trillion) and employ 62 percent of the U.S. workforce."[4] The cumulative effect of a large number of preventable business failures every year must have a significant macroeconomic effect.

A 2008 study in the United Kingdom indicated that 30 percent of business failures were due to succession failure.[5] This implies that if business owners did a better job of planning their own succession, this would also be in the public interest from the point of view of maximizing gross domestic product (GDP) and employment growth. Most job creation occurs at the level of small and medium-sized companies. In every country there must be a few hundred or a few thousand firms, like my father's, that might have been saved with better exit planning. When a firm disappears from the marketplace, the slack is very quickly taken up by competitors, yet we can only speculate about whether an improvement in exit planning might lead to GDP or employment growth at a rate of 1 or 2 percent faster than might otherwise occur. A lack of Business Exit Planning simply vaporizes a significant portion of each country's GDP every year!

Take the Schumpeterian view of business succession: it is a natural part of the free market system to have all this creative destruction going on.[6] But I'm not sure what purpose it serves. And it is not evident whether the slack taken up by the bankruptcy of a company will be taken up by local or foreign competitors.

> There is potential for a major growth industry here over the coming decade that could help contain the number of exit and succession failures.

Rather than relying on the government to fix the problem (although sponsoring awareness and training programs might marginally help), I see improvement coming from two sources. First, consulting and financial advisory firms can play a significant role in catalyzing Business Exit Planning. There is potential for a major growth industry here over the coming decade that could help contain the number of exit and succession failures. But the ultimate responsibility for organizing your own exit and succession is with you, the business owner.

Your ownership in a privately held company is a highly illiquid investment. A very optimistic scenario is that you might be able to exit within eight to 12 months of making your decision, but the real figure is more like one to three years, assuming market conditions and the condition of your business are both good.

The value of your company is purely theoretical, until you unlock that value via a Transaction. If you have exited on terms and a price satisfactory to yourself, that is when you can truly call your investment of time and money in your business a success, an *éxito*, as the Spanish would say.

# Notes

## Introduction: The Challenge of Exiting Your Business

1. Nelson Economic Development Partnership. 2008. *Nelson Business Succession Survey.* Available at: http://www.futures.bc.ca/documents/businesssuccessionreportnovember2008.pdf.
2. Leonetti, J.M. 2007. *Exiting your Business, Protecting your Wealth.* John Wiley & Sons: Hoboken, NJ.
3. Trump, D, and T. Schwartz. 1989. *The Art of the Deal.* Warner: New York.

## CHAPTER 1    An Introduction to Business Exit Planning

1. Maru, K, and R.A. Prince. 1996. Attributions for family business failure: The heir's perspective. *Family Business Review* 9(2): 171–184.
2. Jackim, R, and P. Christman. 2005. *The $10 Trillion Opportunity.* Dog Ear Publishing: Indianapolis, IN.
3. Nelson Economic Development Partnership (2008) *op. cit.*
4. Jackim and Christman (2005) *op. cit.*
5. Coutts & Co. 2009. *The Long Goodbye: Myths, Realities and Insights into the Business Exit Process.* Coutts: London. Available at: http://www.coutts.co.uk/files/Business_Exit_Report_-_The_Long_Goodbye.pdf.
6. Leonetti (2007) *op. cit.*
7. KPMG. 2006. *Selling up is not hard to do.* KPMG LLP, London. Available at: http://www.kpmg.is/media/fyrirtaekjasvid/Sellin_up_is_not_so_hard_to_do.pdf.
8. CPA Institute of Australia. 2004. *Small Business Survey: Succession and Exits.* Available at: http://www.cpaaustralia.com.au/cps/rde/xchg/SID-3F57FEDF-DF8AC16/cpa/hs.xsl/726_7914_ENA_HTML.htm [10 February 2010].

## CHAPTER 2    Begin with the Endgame in Sight

1. Jackim and Christman (2005) *op. cit.*

## CHAPTER 3    Exit Options

1. Robbins, D. 2008. *Tales from the Trenches of a Business Intermediary.* Robbinex: Ontario, Canada.
2. CPA Institute of Australia (2004) *op. cit.*

## CHAPTER 5    Building a Business with Sustainable Value

1. AmCham Hungary. 2005. Good Corporate Governance as a Pillar of Hungarian National Competitiveness: Leading to Better Decisions, Increased

Valuations & More Investment, AmCham Hungary Position Brief No. 5. American Chamber of Commerce: Budapest, Hungary.

## CHAPTER 6    Business Plan and Valuation

1. American Society of Appraisers. 2006. *Business Valuations 201N: Introduction to Business Valuation*, ASA: Atlanta, GA.
2. Harvard Business School Press. 2001. *Harvard Business Review on Mergers and Acquisitions*, Harvard Business School Press: Boston.
3. Another one bites the dust. *The Economist*. January 21, 2010. Available at: http://www.economist.com/world/britain/displaystory.cfm?story_id= 15331177.

## CHAPTER 9    The Transaction Process

1. Harvard Business School Press (2001) *op. cit.*

## CHAPTER 10    Negotiating a Transaction

1. Fisher, R., W. Ury, and B. Patton. 1999. *Getting to Yes: Negotiating Agreement without Giving in*. Penguin Books: New York.

## CHAPTER 11    Cross-border Transactions

1. Hofstede, G. 1984. *Culture's Consequences*. Sage Publications: Beverly Hills, CA.
2. *Ibid.*
3. Hi there—Life is getting friendlier but less interesting. Blame technology, globalisation and feminism. *The Economist*. December 19, 2009. Available at: http://www.economist.com/research/articlesBySubject/displaystory.cfm? subjectid=423172&story_id=15108779.

## Conclusion: The Only Question with Wealth Is, What Do You Do with It?

1. Grothe, M. 2004. *Oxymoronica: Paradoxical Wit & Wisdom from History's Greatest Wordsmiths*. Harper: New York.
2. Trillion-dollar babies. A fast-growing asset class. *The Economist*, January 23, 2010. Available at: http://www.economist.com/businessfinance/displaystory .cfm?story_id=15331133.
3. Ibid.
4. Astrachan, J, and M.C. Shanker. 2003. Family businesses' contribution to the U.S. economy: A closer look. *Family Business Review*. 16(3): 211–219.
5. Nelson Economic Development Partnership (2008) *op. cit.*
6. Schumpeter, J. 1942. *Capitalism, Socialism, and Democracy*. Harper & Row: New York.

# Glossary

**Business Exit:** Refers to the transfer of ownership as well as leadership or governance of a business, usually in the context of a Transaction that brings liquidity to the exiting owner(s) of a business. Business Exit may include the sale of a business, an Initial Public Offering, a Management Buyout, or an Intergenerational Transfer.

**Business Exit Planning:** The process of explicitly defining exit-related objectives for the owner(s) of a business, followed by the design of a comprehensive strategy and road map that take into account all personal, business, financial, legal, and taxation aspects of achieving those objectives, usually in the context of planning the leadership succession and continuity of a business. Objectives may include maximizing (or setting a goal for) proceeds, minimizing risk, closing a Transaction quickly, or selecting an investor that will ensure that the business prospers. The strategy should also take into account contingencies such as illness or death.

**Buy-Sell Agreement:** An agreement between two or more shareholders whereby an event of default by one shareholder (such as death or disability) triggers the obligation of the other shareholder(s) to buy out the defaulting shareholder.

**Call Option:** The right of a party to buy specific assets, shares or other rights at a stated price for a stated period. The holder of the Call Option may exercise the call for the stated price within the stated period.

**Control Premium:** A price premium that a willing purchaser would offer to pay for the right to exercise effective control over a company or other business organization.

**Data Room:** The process of setting out all original documents that may materially impact the valuation and level of risk in a business, including contracts, title documents, permits, and financial records.

**Discounted Cash Flow (DCF):** DCF, also known as a present value analysis, is an approach to estimating the current value of an income-producing asset by calculating the present value of a projected future income stream with the use of an appropriate discount rate, the Weighted Average Cost of Capital (WACC).

**Due Diligence:** In this book, I refer to Due Diligence as comprising three events: first, the holding of a Data Room; second, the holding of one or more Management Presentations; and third, the conducting of site visits. Due Diligence may also be described as the process by which one or more investors investigate the original source documents in a company in order to provide a binding offer.

**Earn-Out:** An agreement between a seller and a purchaser of a business as to the payment of the purchase price in which the purchaser agrees to pay a substantial sum at first closing and pay additional consideration at one or more subsequent closings, based on the actual future earnings of the business sold.

**Heads of Agreement:** See *Term Sheet.*

**Heads of Terms:** See *Term Sheet.*

**Information Memorandum (IM):** A document that sets out the material information an investor needs to know about a company, typically in order to make a non-binding offer. Some jurisdictions require that an Information Memorandum contain full, true, and plain disclosure on all facts which may materially influence the value of the company.

**Initial Public Offering (IPO):** The process of listing a company on a stock exchange and selling shares to the general public.

**Intergenerational Transfer:** The transfer of ownership and governance of a company to one or more of the children or next-of-kin of the owner(s).

**Internal Rate of Return (IRR):** The annualized effective compounded return rate that is earned on capital invested. IRR is calculated as the discount rate that makes the net present value of all cash flows from a particular investment project equal to zero.

**Management Buyout (MBO):** The acquisition of a company by its existing managers, typically a leveraged transaction, which often uses as collateral the assets and/or future cash flow of the company.

**Management Presentation:** A presentation given to investors by management, usually at the first encounter between investors and the management team as part of a Due Diligence process.

**Process Letter:** A letter that sets out the deadline for submitting offers, the form and substance of the offer, along with any rules to be followed during the bid process.

**Put Option:** The duty of a party to sell specific assets, shares, or other rights at a stated price for a stated period. The holder of a Put Option may exercise it for the stated price within the stated period.

**Representations and Warranties:** Statements and guarantees by a seller of a business relating to the assets, liabilities, and contacts of the business sold. The breach of such Representations and Warranties may result in damages payable by the seller to the purchaser. There are usually also less extensive Representations and Warranties given by an investor to the seller of a business.

**Sale and Purchase Agreement (SPA):** The legal agreement that sets out all of the parameters of a Transaction.

**Shareholders' Agreement:** An agreement by and among the shareholders (owners) of a company pertaining to the governance of the company, the specific rights of the shareholders, and the duties of the shareholders regarding competition with the company, as well as restrictions on the transfer of the shareholders' equity interests.

**Teaser:** A short investment summary on a company for sale or seeking to raise capital that is widely circulated to potential investors, to ascertain which investors may be interested.

**Term Sheet:** An agreement that summarizes the main commercial terms of a Transaction. It may be either binding or non-binding. A Term Sheet is similar in meaning to *Heads of Agreement* or *Heads of Terms*. A Term Sheet is sometimes entered into before granting exclusivity to one investor, or as a condition for either allowing an investor into a Data Room or for entering into negotiations with respect to an SPA.

**Transaction:** A transfer of at least partial ownership in a company, for due consideration.

**Transaction Management:** The process of managing a Transaction, from the perspective of a business owner.

**Vendor Due Diligence:** A process whereby a company requests its own advisors to evaluate all information in the Data Room, from the perspective of an investor, prior to opening the Data Room to investors. A Vendor Due Diligence may be used for internal purposes by a business owner (e.g. to anticipate possible issues that may arise during Due Diligence) or it may be shared with potential investors to expedite their own Due Diligence process.

**Vendor Financing:** A process whereby a seller of a business takes back debt or accepts deferred compensation from the purchaser, as a means of financing the purchase price.

**Weighted Average Cost of Capital (WACC):** The rate that a company is expected to pay on average to all its security holders to finance its assets; that is, a calculation of the overall cost of capital used by a company, made by multiplying the cost of each source of capital used by its proportional share of the total capital used, then adding the resulting figures.

# References

Cohen, H. 1982. *You Can Negotiate Anything*. Bantam Books: New York.

Crozier, L.P. 2004. *Selling Your Business, The Transition from Entrepreneur to Investor*. John Wiley and Sons, Hoboken, NJ.

Dawson, R. 1999. *Secrets of Power Negotiating*. Career Press: Franklin Lakes, NJ.

Depree, M. 1990. *Leadership is an Art*. Dell: New York.

Garrison, P. 2006. *Exponential Marketing*. HVG Kiadó: Budapest, Hungary.

Hamel, C, and C.K. Prahalad. 1989. *Competing for the Future*. Harvard Business Press: Boston.

Hammer, M, and J. Champy. 1994. *Re-Engineering the Corporation: A Manifesto for Business Revolution*. HarperBusiness: New York.

Handy, C. 1995. *Gods of Management: The Changing Work of Organizations*. Oxford University Press: New York.

Kim, C, and R. Mauborgne. 2005. *Blue Ocean Strategy*. Harvard Business School Press: Boston.

Merrill Lynch. 2006. The 2006 Merrill Lynch New Retirement Study. Available at: http://www.ml.com/media/66482.pdf.

Metz, T. Jr. 2009. *Selling the Intangible Company, How to Negotiate and Capture the Value of a Growth Firm*. John Wiley & Sons: Hoboken, NJ.

Rickersten, R. 2006. *Selling Your Business Your Way*. AMACOM: New York.

Sherman, A. 1998. *Mergers and Acquisitions from A to Z—Strategic and Practical Guidance for Buyers and Sellers*. AMACOM: New York.

Treen, D. 2009. *Psychology of Executive Retirement from Fear to Passion*. iUniverse, Inc.: New York.

Trottier, R.M. 2009. *Middle Market Strategies, How Private Companies Use the Market to Create Value*. John Wiley & Sons: Hoboken, NJ.

Weston, F, and E. Brigham. 1986. *Managerial Finance*. Saunders College Publishing/ Harcourt Brace: Philadelphia.

# About the Author

In a career spanning 25 years, Les Nemethy has been involved in the sale of hundreds of businesses, large and small, in more than 40 countries. Founder and CEO of Euro-Phoenix Financial Advisors Ltd. (www .europhoenix.com) —a leading corporate finance house in emerging markets specializing in helping owners of mid-sized enterprises sell their companies—Nemethy has distilled decades of experience into this very readable book, aimed at assisting business owners to first plan for their business exits, and then manage the exit process.

Nemethy has seen the process of buying and selling companies from just about every perspective—buyer, seller, financial advisor, legal advisor, and banker. After obtaining degrees in economics, law, international relations, and business administration from leading Canadian universities, Nemethy worked with a major Canadian law firm, McMillan Binch, and was called to the Ontario Bar in 1984. He then worked for the Canadian investment bank, McLeod Young Weir (today ScotiaMcLeod). His career took an eclectic turn in early 1992, when he was named head of the Transactions Department of the Hungarian Privatization Agency. Leading a team of 150 professional staff, Nemethy contributed to the ramping up of the privatization program, with more than 6000 companies sold during his tenure. He led the privatization of the telecom incumbent, of gas distribution companies, and numerous breweries, hotels, cement companies, and so on. He also led a number of Initial Public Offerings (IPOs) on the Budapest Stock Exchange.

Nemethy moved from Hungary to Washington DC in July 1993, where he worked with the World Bank, helping governments in 23 countries privatize companies and attract investment. For example, he helped the Kuwait Investment Authority devise a program to sell approximately $6 billion of assets on the Kuwait Stock Exchange; he advised the governments of Cote d'Ivoire, Sri Lanka, and Albania on managing their national privatization programs; and he was part of a team assisting the Russian Privatization Centre with a $277 million loan.

In 1997, Nemethy became CEO of MaTel, the second-largest telecom operator in Hungary (today Invitel). In this capacity, he also worked on a number of acquisitions, before founding Euro-Phoenix in 2000. Currently based in Budapest, Hungary, Nemethy lectures frequently and has taught courses in universities from Georgetown University to the Central European University, mostly on the subject of negotiations. Former President of the American Chamber of Commerce in Budapest, his incisive commentaries on Central European finance and business issues regularly feature in regional and international press on radio and TV.

# Index

Printed and bound by CPI Group (UK) Ltd, Croydon, CR0 4YY

16/04/2025

14658454-0001